Assessing European Neighbourhood Policy

Assessing European Neighbourhood Policy

Perspectives from the literature

Study commissioned by the Policy and Operations Evaluation Department of the Ministry of Foreign Affairs of the Netherlands

Edited by

Hrant Kostanyan

Contributors

Steven Blockmans

Hrant Kostanyan

Artem Remizov

Linda Slapakova

Guillaume Van der Loo

CEPS, Brussels
Rowman and Littlefield International, London

Published by Rowman & Littlefield International, Ltd.
Unit A, Whitacre Mews, 26-34 Stannary Street, London SE11 4AB
www.rowmaninternational.com

Rowman & Littlefield International Ltd. is an affiliate of Rowman &
Littlefield
4501 Forbes Boulevard, Suite 200, Lanham, Maryland 20706, USA
With additional offices in Boulder, New York, Toronto (Canada), and
Plymouth (UK)
www.rowman.com

Centre for European Policy Studies (CEPS)
Place du Congrès 1, 1000 Brussels, Belgium
www.ceps.eu

The authors have asserted their rights to be identified as the authors of
this work in accordance with the Copyright, Designs and Patents Act
1988.

British Library Cataloguing in Publication Data
A catalogue record for this book is available from the British Library

ISBN: 978-1-78660-444-6 Hardback
        978-1-78660-445-3 Paperback
        978-1-78660-446-0 Ebook

⊖™ The paper used in this publication meets the minimum
requirements of American National Standard for Information
Sciences—Permanence of Paper for Printed Library Materials,
ANSI/NISO Z39.48-1992.

Printed in the United States of America

CONTENTS

LIST OF ABBREVIATIONS

ACP	Africa, Caribbean and Pacific
CFSP	Common Foreign and Security Policy
CIS	Commonwealth of Independent States
COEST	Working Party on Eastern Europe and Central Asia
COREPER	Committee of Permanent Representatives in the Council of the European Union
CSDP	Common Security and Defence Policy
DCFTA	Deep and comprehensive free trade area
DG	Directorate-general
DG DEVCO	Directorate-General for International Cooperation and Development
DG ECHO	Directorate-General for European Civil Protection and Humanitarian Aid Operations
DG ENER	Directorate-General for Energy
DG HOME	Directorate-General for Home Affairs
DG NEAR	Directorate-General for Neighbourhood and Enlargement Negotiations
EAEU	Eurasian Economic Union
EaP	Eastern Partnership
EEAS	European External Action Service
ENP	European Neighbourhood Policy
EuroNest PA	EU–Eastern Partnership Parliamentary Assembly
EUSR	European Union special representative
HR/VP	High Representative of the Union for Foreign Affairs and Security Policy and Vice-President of the European Commission
IOB	Policy and Operations Evaluation Department, Ministry of Foreign Affairs of the Netherlands

MENA	Middle East and North Africa
NATO	North Atlantic Treaty Organization
OSCE	Organization for Security and Cooperation in Europe
PCA	Partnership and cooperation agreement
TEU	Treaty on the European Union
TFEU	Treaty on the Functioning of the European Union
TNC	Transitional National Council (of Libya)
UAE	United Arab Emirates
V4	Visegrad Four

ABOUT THE AUTHORS

Hrant Kostanyan is Researcher at CEPS, a Senior Key Expert at the College of Europe Natolin and an Adjunct Professor at Vesalius College.

Steven Blockmans is Senior Research Fellow and the Head of the EU Foreign Policy unit of CEPS and a Professor of EU External Relations Law and Governance, University of Amsterdam.

Artem Remizov is Visiting Fellow at CEPS and Erasmus Mundus PhD Fellow (LUISS Guido Carli/ULB).

Linda Slapakova is an Intern at CEPS and the President of Vesalius Student Government, Vesalius College.

Guillaume Van der Loo is Researcher at CEPS and a postdoctoral researcher (FWO) at the Ghent European Law Institute (GELI).

FOREWORD

The European Neighbourhood Policy (ENP) is a key priority within the European Union's foreign policy. Many events in the past few years have shown that the interests of European citizens are directly affected by the stability, security and prosperity of the European Union's neighbouring regions. At the same time, the Union and its member states face many challenges and dilemmas in designing and pursuing a policy that not only effectively promotes these interests, but also builds stronger partnerships with the neighbouring countries based on the values on which the Union is founded.

The Ministry of Foreign Affairs of the Netherlands is committed to contributing to a more effective, efficient and coherent foreign policy of the European Union. In light of this commitment, the Policy and Operations Evaluation Department (IOB) has embarked upon a policy evaluation of the Netherlands' contribution to the ENP, focusing on these three dimensions. Apart from providing public accountability for the policy pursued, this evaluation aims to draw lessons for the future.

The IOB has commissioned this literature review, performed by CEPS in Brussels, as one of the building blocks of its policy evaluation. The academic literature on the ENP is extensive and multidisciplinary, dating back to the policy's inception in 2003. First the Arab revolts and then Russia's assertiveness in the eastern neighbourhood prompted reviews of the ENP, in 2011 and 2015 respectively. These reviews have renewed scholarly interest in the ENP. However, despite a rapidly growing body of literature, there was no systematic review available that catalogued and assessed the explanatory variables used by ENP scholars.

By focusing on the recent literature (since 2011), this review by CEPS deliberately identifies the factors that explain the (lack of) effectiveness and coherence of the ENP. This exercise has resulted in a rich overview of and informed reflection on a wide variety of

ENP-related themes. The study identifies where there is consensus among scholars and where perspectives and judgement differ. It also identifies several gaps in the literature where further research is needed.

By publishing this study, IOB and CEPS aim to enrich the ongoing debate on the ENP among both academics and policy-makers. It is of interest to a wide audience of officials, diplomats, parliamentarians, researchers at think tanks, civil society organisations, university teachers, trainers, students and journalists who want to know more about the ENP.

The study was prepared by a team of researchers from CEPS in Brussel and was edited by Hrant Kostanyan, researcher at CEPS. During the drafting phase, it has benefitted from the comments by IOB evaluators Bas Limonard, Tim Scheerder and Paul de Nooijer. The views in this book are entirely those of the authors and should not be attributed to CEPS, IOB or the Ministry of Foreign Affairs of the Netherlands.

This book is available in both print and in PDF. It can be downloaded freely from https://english.iob-evaluatie.nl and www.ceps.eu.

Dr. Wendy Asbeek Brusse

Director Policy and Operations Evaluation Department (IOB)

Ministry of Foreign Affairs of the Netherlands

SUMMARY

This report presents a review of the literature on the European Neighbourhood Policy (ENP) published since 2011. Through the application of an iterative research design, the review aims to identify the main factors contributing to the effectiveness of the ENP and the levels for assessing its coherence as selected and applied in the literature. From their review of the literature, the authors identify six major factors determining the effectiveness of the ENP, namely conditionality and socialisation, interests and values, ownership and local dynamics, the visibility and perceptions of the ENP, the influence of external (f)actors and coherence.

Scholars pay considerable attention to conditionality when addressing the effectiveness of the ENP. The literature on conditionality tends to focus on the analysis of democracy promotion by the EU. The EU seeks to transfer its values to the neighbouring countries not only through conditionality, but also through the use of linkages and functional cooperation. The effectiveness of conditionality as a mechanism for democratisation, however, has been limited. This is the result of a combination of factors: the EU's conditions have not been well defined, the EU has shown a lack of determination and political will in the pursuit of its approach and its offer has been of limited interest to the partners.

The literature extensively debates the limits of the EU's conditionality in particular because of its flawed design and implementation. The differentiation introduced by the 2015 Review of the ENP is likely to complicate the application of conditionality. Finally, analysis of the eastern dimension of the ENP pays particular attention to the lack of membership prospects in the ENP, which is often cited as one of the major limitations of the policy.

Despite the fact that the EU is built on a solid normative foundation that also extends to its foreign policy activities, the literature overwhelmingly argues that the EU in most cases follows its own pragmatic interests rather than its core values when dealing with ENP states. Yet, as a policy framework, the ENP serves the EU's interest in pursuing its main goal – to guarantee the security of its own citizens – by trying to create a ring of stable and well-governed states around its borders.

According to the literature, a number of reasons explain why the EU gives preference to security when faced with an interests-vs-values dilemma. First, the values fixed by the EU's legal body are ill-defined and ambiguous in their nature, which consequently leads to a conflict between them. Second, the vagueness of objectives and values results in a fuzziness of benchmarks with which the ENP partners have to comply. Therefore, it provides the opportunity for the EU and its member states to interpret the objectives in different ways. Third, there is no clear prioritisation of the various goals, normative or realist, which allows the EU to choose objectives on an ad hoc basis, depending on what it finds most appropriate in each particular case.

Indeed, there is a gap in the literature on interests vs. values as far as decision-making in the EU is concerned. The EU is often treated as a unitary actor, whereas the interests within the EU are diverse. Aside from the lack of clarity in EU values, it is the combination of the individual interests and preferences of member states that shape the EU's choices in the neighbourhood.

The lack of local ownership and consideration of local needs and conditions constitutes one of the aspects of the ENP on which there is consensus across the reviewed academic literature. One can debate the extent to which the ENP allows for shared or joint ownership while keeping a focus on both positive and negative conditionality. Nevertheless, with regard to political as well as economic reforms, liberalisation and democratisation, it is clear that more differentiation is needed to reflect the diverse nature of local conditions and experiences in the neighbourhood. High politics, such as national security and migration, will most likely continue to define the agenda for the EU's relationship with the neighbourhood countries. If the ENP is to achieve its goals in regional development and democratisation, then a focus on local experiences and perspectives is needed to shape a successful policy that works for the ENP countries as much as it does for the EU.

There are different perceptions of the ENP both within and outside the EU. In spite of the relatively positive image of the EU within societies of the neighbouring states, the southern neighbours do not perceive themselves as equal partners. Moreover, the ENP does not meet the expectations of the Eastern Partnership states either, particularly when it comes to the prospect of membership and readiness by the EU to contribute in terms of political and economic support.

The dissatisfaction with the ENP might also be explained by problems the EU faces in terms of visibility in the neighbouring states. In particular, information about the EU's programmes and its support for ENP societies and governments is not available to the general public. Thus, there is a significant lack of knowledge about the nature of the EU and its policies within ENP societies, which in turn leads to both positive and negative mythologies about the EU.

As far as external factors are concerned, there is considerably more literature on the eastern neighbourhood then on the southern dimension of the ENP. The 2008 war in Georgia and the recent political events in Ukraine have brought the role of Russia in the eastern neighbourhood into the spotlight of ENP research. The literature addressing the eastern neighbourhood concentrates on the dynamic between the EU and Russia and the impact of this dynamic on domestic developments as well as domestic policy preferences of the countries of the common neighbourhood. The literature on the southern neighbourhood focuses on the relationship between the ENP and the EU's wider regional policy frameworks.

With regard to the eastern neighbourhood, the literature analyses the role of Russia as an external actor in the region. First, the extent to which the Russian presence in the region has had an impact on domestic policy preferences and sectoral convergence is unclear. While some authors suggest that political and economic pressure from the Kremlin has in several instances precluded countries in the eastern neighbourhood from pursuing deeper integration with the EU, others suggest that political and economic interdependencies with Russia have constituted a positive factor in convergence with EU policies. Second, there are disagreements as to what constitutes the basis for the current nature of Russian foreign policy and engagement in the region. While some argue that

Russia has actively developed an assertive foreign policy based on its strategic considerations, others see this development merely as a response to the expansion of the EU's presence in the region.

Several aspects, including the impact of the involvement of global actors like China and the US in the southern neighbourhood, are under-researched. Certainly, external factors such as migratory pressures, rising security threats from terrorism and Islamic radicalisation have affected the application of the ENP in the southern neighbourhood. At the same time, what is less clear are the ways in which the rapidly changing, post-Arab Spring geopolitical environment in the Middle East and the war in Syria influence the role of external actors in the southern neighbourhood, such as Iran and the Gulf states.

Because coherence is a very broad and fuzzy concept, often differently interpreted by legal and political science scholars, this review of ENP literature conceptualises coherence at three interrelated levels: i) horizontal (among different EU policies and instruments), ii) vertical (between the EU and its member states) and iii) institutional (between and within the EU institutions).

The literature is overwhelmingly critical about horizontal coherence in the ENP. The various ENP instruments are generally not perceived as being mutually reinforcing of the different ENP policy objectives. It was also noted that the EU's ability to promote coherence among its instruments depends on the domestic situation in the ENP country in question. The more stable, democratic and 'EU-friendly' the ENP country is, the more coherent can be the EU's deployment of its instruments. There is also a broad consensus on the lack of coherence among the assorted ENP objectives. In particular, it appears that the EU has preferred its 'stabilisation' objective to the 'democratisation' objective in its reaction to the Arab Spring.

Also, the degree of vertical coherence has proved to be insufficient. EU member states were not capable of 'speaking with one voice' in the context of the Arab Spring. Whereas it is recognised that the EU member states swiftly agreed to adopt sanctions against Russia for its role in the Ukraine crisis, several authors doubt whether the member states will be able to extend the sanctions in the future, even if the Minsk agreements are not entirely implemented.

The literature is more positive with regard to the EU's intra- and inter-institutional coherence. Although the collaboration between the European External Action Service (EEAS) and the Commission in the area of the ENP is highly complex, there is a consensus in the literature that it has proven to work rather well. Still, the coordination between the EEAS and different Commission directorates-general could be improved. The discretionary power of the EEAS is limited in the ENP, as illustrated during the negotiations on the association agreements, because its activities are closely monitored and controlled by the member states.

Most authors also claim that coherence is a precondition for an effective ENP. This claim should not be overstated, however, because even if the EU's ENP instruments and objectives are coherent, there is no guarantee that the EU's approach will prompt the desired effect.

The 2015 ENP Review demonstrates that the EU is shifting towards a more realist, pragmatic and flexible approach towards its neighbourhood. Hence, the ENP first of all is framed as a stabilisation instrument. Despite several significant innovations to make the ENP a more flexible and responsive policy, the prevalence of strategic interests on the EU's agenda and the readiness to downgrade its normative component represent a shift to a more traditional foreign policy thought to still contain some normative elements. Naturally, this raises legitimate concerns among the pro-European democratic segments of ENP societies. At the same time, further evolution of the ENP will depend on actual policy steps and decisions made by the EU and its member states in each particular case.

With increased differentiation, there is a risk that the promotion of stability and security will be prioritised at the cost of democratisation. Moreover, the shift towards stabilisation can also indirectly contribute to the affirmation of undemocratic regimes in the EU's neighbourhood. The ENP review does not acknowledge or address this paradox. A way forward for the EU could be to identify a key set of democratic principles and values, for example by referring to internationally recognised values enshrined in international agreements and conventions, that are considered as the threshold above which the joint ownership principle can operate.

The 2015 Review of the ENP does address the wish voiced by a growing number of local stakeholders to see security matters incorporated to a limited extent into the ENP framework. For example, the new ENP addresses Russia's assertive policies in the neighbourhood, but only by making vague commitments to strengthen the resilience of the partners that suffered the most from such policies. Ultimately, the 2015 Review does not provide a strategic vision for the EU's relations with its neighbours, but rather focuses on the short-term challenges.

Finally, scholars often show a bias towards analysing certain topics (e.g. geopolitics), variables (e.g. interests vs values) and countries (e.g. Ukraine). The EU is viewed as a normative actor and a promoter of democracy and human rights rather than as a provider of security and stability to the neighbourhood seeking to counter the spillovers that negatively affect its citizens. There are both consensus and divergence with regard to the independent variables and, in a number of instances, one finds an overlap between them and the way in which they are used in the literature. When dealing with the explanatory variables, ENP scholars in many cases 'compartmentalise' rather than combine different variables. Such approaches, along with the challenging situation on the ground in many neighbourhood countries, explain the general negative attitude in the literature vis-à-vis the effectiveness of the ENP.

1. INTRODUCTION

The academic literature on the European Neighbourhood Policy (ENP) is extensive and multidisciplinary, dating back to the policy's inception in 2003. First the Arab revolts and then Russia's assertiveness in the eastern neighbourhood prompted reviews of the ENP, in 2011 and 2015 respectively, and have renewed scholarly interest in the ENP. However, despite the availability of a rapidly growing body of literature, there is currently no systematic review that problematises concepts, and catalogues and assesses the explanatory variables used by the ENP scholars. By focusing on the recent literature (since 2011) that has strong empirical foundations, this review addresses the following research questions:

1.   How does the literature conceptualise the effectiveness and coherence of the ENP?

2.   To what extent does the literature consider the ENP to be effective and coherent?

3.   What factors are identified in the literature that explain the effectiveness and coherence of the ENP?

In problematising effectiveness, this review concentrates on the link between the EU's interventions (output level) and their contributions to the ENP (outcome level). In doing so, the review does not pretend to be able to evaluate the effectiveness of the EU in achieving the *general* goals of the ENP, namely stability, security and prosperity. Because of the often broad and vague nature of the policy goals of the ENP, establishing clear causal relations between output and outcome levels is not plausible. Furthermore, distinguishing between the EU's influence and other exogenous and indigenous factors (e.g. water scarcity in the Middle East and North Africa, MENA), or actors that may and do account for the state of stability, security and prosperity in the neighbourhood countries (e.g. Russia) is not realistic within the framework of this literature review. Instead, this report focuses on the main factors outlined by the existing literature that aim to explain the EU's effectiveness.

1.1 Conceptualising and assessing the effectiveness and coherence of the ENP

Although the ENP has attracted considerable interest among scholars, its theorisation remains underdeveloped. First, there has been no effort at theory-building through analysis of the ENP. Second, existing theories of political science, international relations and EU studies have been applied to the ENP, but to a limited extent. A recent effort to theorise the ENP was led by Gstöhl and Schunz (2016) in their edited volume, which applies mainstream and critical theories going beyond EU-centric approaches. The authors apply rationalism and constructivism to the study of the ENP, and use insights from the new institutionalism, post-structuralism and inter-regionalism. Such theorisation facilitates understanding of the ENP, though it does not seek to offer immediate solutions to the challenges that the policy faces.

Moreover, even in theoretically-driven literature, the ENP is not framed from the perspective of effectiveness. The screening of the literature reveals that scholars distinguish mainly among six main factors that provide information on the (in)effectiveness of the ENP. These are 1) the application of conditionality, 2) tensions between interests and values, 3) the level of local dynamics and local ownership, 4) the visibility and perceptions of the ENP, 5) the influence of external (f)actors and 6) coherence.

Conditionality is one of the most studied factors in relation to the effectiveness of the ENP, particularly in its goal to promote democracy in the neighbourhood. Conditionality is described as the EU's ability to attach specific demands to incentives it offers to the neighbours. This includes sanctioning or rewarding neighbours, as well as creating and applying leverage (e.g. legal reform in return for visa liberalisation or financial support on the basis of 'more for more'/'less for less'). There is a general consensus in the literature that the effectiveness of conditionality depends on both the attractiveness and the credibility of the EU's offer, and coordination between the EU and its member states in the implementation of the principle. Particular limitations of the conditionality literature include its bias in favour of the democracy and human rights promotion, its EU-centrism and in some cases neglect of the other (f)actors.

Despite the claim that the EU's interests (e.g. security and stability) and values (e.g. respect for democracy and human rights) may at times coincide, the EU often prioritises one over the other when tensions arise between them. The literature focusing on the interests-vs-values dilemma argues that the EU tends to give priority to such strategic objectives as the maintenance of regional security and stability, while the promotion of democracy and other EU values takes place only when it does not impede the EU's efforts to reach the former two goals. Thus, the majority of the authoritarian leaders who govern in the neighbouring states are viewed as undesirable but necessary partners in pursuing the aforementioned goals. As a result, the EU opts for functional cooperation with those regimes in a limited number of sectors rather than taking a firm position on their compliance with democratic and human rights standards. Consequently, it is suggested that such a stance undermines the EU's image as a normative power, both domestically and internationally, and hinders its capability to effectively employ conditionality in the neighbourhood. The interests-vs.-values debate as examined in the present literature would benefit from acknowledging the diversity within the EU rather than treating it as unitary actor. Taking into account the individual preferences of the EU member states and the way in which they utilise the decision-making processes to advance their own interests could enrich the debate and bring more depth and balance to it.

The EU-centrism of the ENP and lack of ownership by the neighbours in defining and implementing the policy is another area of contention often cited as a factor in the ineffectiveness of the ENP. The literature is inconclusive on whether the disregard for local conditions can be explained by a lack of understanding of these conditions or rather a strategic prioritisation on the part of the EU of its own interests and perspectives. It is not clear to what extent it is feasible to suggest that the EU will find a way to direct the ENP towards the needs of local communities and civil society in an environment increasingly defined by domestic security concerns triggered by instability and the migration crisis, especially in the MENA region. There is, however, a consensus in the literature that such a transition to focusing on the local needs will be needed to stimulate further political reforms and contribute to democratisation in the neighbourhood.

An analysis of the visibility and perceptions of the ENP includes an assessment of the gap between the EU's rhetoric and the realities on the ground. Some neighbouring states, especially in the east, have much higher expectations of the ENP than what is on offer. The southern neighbours in particular do not view the relationship with the EU as symmetrical. Efforts at improving perceptions about the EU are also tied to the need to enhance communication about the EU's nature and the visibility of its policies in the neighbourhood.

The proliferation of the literature on the external (f)actors in recent years is the result of acknowledgement that the EU is far from the only game in town. The external factors contributing to or hindering the effectiveness of the ENP include not only contestation by Russia or the neighbours of the EU's southern ENP countries (e.g. Iran and Saudi Arabia), but also refugee flows and migratory pressures, economic imbalances and unemployment, climate change, Islamic radicalisation and terrorism. On balance, scholars have paid more attention to the eastern neighbourhood and Russia than to the southern neighbourhood. Whereas Russia presents a challenge geopolitically, its effect on EU-driven domestic reforms in the Eastern Partnership (EaP) countries is not clear-cut. The Gulf states, refugee crisis and terrorism are increasingly factored in the analysis of the EU's relations with the southern neighbours.

Whether coherence constitutes a precondition for the principle of effectiveness remains subject to discussion. This report understands coherence as a predisposition towards collaborative and mutually reinforcing positions and actions of multiple actors. Yet, going beyond the concept of consistency (i.e. a lack of contradiction), this literature review operationalises 'synergetic' coherence of the ENP at four interrelated levels, namely horizontal (i.e. among EU policies and their goals), vertical (i.e. between the EU and its member states) and institutional (i.e. between and within the EU institutions). In relation to vertical coherence, the report analyses not only the coherence between the policies of the member states and those of the EU, but also their individual preferences. Although the EU foreign policy literature further features multilateral coherence (i.e. within multilateral fora), this study did not find any significant contributions concerning multilateral coherence with regard to the ENP.

On balance, the literature is negative concerning the effectiveness of the EU's policies in its neighbourhood. When assessing the effectiveness of the ENP, the literature mostly points to the challenges and limitations that the EU faces in the neighbourhood. The literature favours some explanatory valuables, topics, countries and events while discriminating against others. In many cases scholars focus on a few variables rather than reflect a whole host of variables that explain the effectiveness of the ENP. For example, much of the literature argues that the weakness of conditionality is to blame for the lack of progress in democratisation of the neighbourhood. The (in)effectiveness of the ENP is also attributed to the diverging perceptions within the EU and the neighbouring countries. The EU's inability to gain an in-depth understanding of its neighbouring countries is another matter of concern. Achieving the goals inherent in the ENP is equally related to the extent to which shared and local ownership within the ENP is feasible.

The EU is assumed to be a value-driven actor with a normative agenda for its neighbourhood. Still, the EU's role in safeguarding its citizens from the negative effects of the unstable neighbourhood through supporting stability in the neighbouring countries is under-researched. There is extensive study of democracy promotion, the interests-vs-values dilemma and more recently the Russian factor. Meanwhile, the academic literature is underdeveloped when it comes to the visibility of the ENP and how much the EU member states follow the EU line in their bilateral relations with the neighbourhood countries. In fact, when the EU member states come to an agreement at the EU level on a policy vis-à-vis a neighbourhood country, obliging the EU institutions to follow that particular line but in their bilateral relations neglect that agreement, one could safely assume that the EU's policy with respect to the neighbourhood is condemned to be ineffective. Despite these concerns articulated in the literature, the EU remains an attractive partner for most of the countries in its neighbourhood.

1.2 Work/research methods and plan

The design of the evaluation and its corresponding methodological framework is about understanding what elements of the ENP work, and under which conditions, so that patterns can be identified, relationships understood, and lessons can be drawn and applied to future support efforts under the umbrella of the ENP. An ulterior goal of the literature review concerns improving interventions by the EU's institutions and member states.

Methodologically, this literature review follows the logic of *iterative research design*. The research started from an elaboration of the conceptual framework, i.e. result levels and coherence dimensions for assessing the ENP, in close cooperation with the Policy and Operations Evaluation Department (IOB) of the Dutch Ministry of Foreign Affairs. This was followed by an in-depth analysis of the literature. The empirical findings from the literature were then incorporated into the conceptual framework. To assess the strength of the arguments made in the literature, the review relies on the *triangulation* of the data collected from multiple sources, namely English language academic articles, books, think tank and (where relevant) commissioned reports.

The project was executed in four phases. First, during the collection and classification of the relevant literature, the CEPS team identified key sources of literature on the ENP, namely, academic and policy-oriented articles, studies and books. Second, as a part of the inception report CEPS' researchers adopted and applied the evaluation framework introduced in the proposal to the analysis of the literature identified at the first stage. Third, the drafting phase brought together the information from the analysis of the literature into a logical narrative that allows for evaluative conclusions in relation to each of the objectives and research questions. In a fourth and final stage, the study was finalised taking into account any feedback from the project's steering committee and the IOB.

1.3 Data collection strategy

The bulk of the reviewed literature originates from so-called A1 and A2 English language journals, academic books from quality publishers and working papers of highly-rated think tanks.

A1 academic journals are the world's leading scholarly journals that are included in Journal Citation Reports,[1] which is based on an analysis of citation references, influence and impact. The bibliography of this report includes publications on the ENP by A1 journals.

Academics and universities vaguely define the list of A2 journals. In general terms, these are journals that are double-blind peer-reviewed but are not included in the A1 list.[2] The CEPS team tackled this list selectively. The bibliography includes important A2 journals such as the *European Foreign Affairs Review*. In the inception phase, the CEPS team conducted a further search for A2 journals and also looked more carefully for publications on sectoral areas (e.g. CBC, energy, sanitary and phytosanitary, and aviation), regional cooperation (the EaP and Euro-Mediterranean Partnership) and country-specific articles. As a result, the bibliography does not comprise an exhaustive list of articles published in A2 journals but rather a rough selection of publications based on the importance of journals or authors, as judged by the CEPS expert team.

To identify important books, the CEPS team focused on quality publishers, including Palgrave, Routledge, Springer and Brill, and university presses such as Oxford and Cambridge. Besides important academic articles and books the review paid specific attention to in-depth and empirically rich studies of respected think tanks and research institutes. The CEPS team made use of the authoritative "Global Go To Think Tank Index" produced yearly by the University of Pennsylvania.[3] The Index ranks the leading think tanks of the world through the assistance of 1,900 peer institutions and experts from academia, donor institutions, media and governments. The CEPS researchers gave priority to the top think tanks that work on the ENP.

---

[1] See Journal Citation Reports (http://ipscience.thomsonreuters.com/product/journal-citation-reports/?utm_source=false&utm_medium=false&utm_campaign=false&_ga=1.8314164.781882072.146930869).

[2] See Ghent University Academic Bibliography (https://biblio.ugent.be/pages/faq.html).

[3] See Global Go To Think Tank Index (http://gotothinktank.com/).

Another source of both academic and policy publications is the list of the institutions that contributed to the European Union's own ENP Review in 2015. The list was made public by the European Commission.[4]

1.4 Structure

After this introduction, chapter 2 of the literature review focuses on conditionality and socialisation, which covers positive (e.g. membership prospects and visa liberalisation) and negative conditionality (e.g. sanctions), more-for-more and differentiation concepts as well as sectoral cooperation and institutionalisation of the ENP.

Turning to interests vs values, chapter 3 examines the ambiguous nature of values, the dilemma of security/stability vs democracy and (functional) cooperation with non-democratic regimes. Regarding ownership and local dynamics, chapter 4 considers the tailoring of the ENP to local needs, joint and local ownership, civil society support and the Eurocentrism of the ENP. Chapter 5 investigates perceptions and the visibility of the ENP, taking into account views from the EU and the ENP countries, and the EU's communication strategies.

In analysing the external factors in chapter 6, the literature review turns first to the southern neighbourhood, more specifically the role of global and regional actors and that of institutions. Then the eastern neighbourhood is analysed in the context of differing paths of integration, focusing on the case of Ukraine, the EU's normative vs geopolitical actorness and the influence of the EU and Russia on sectoral convergence of the EaP countries. In chapter 7, coherence is assessed through horizontal, vertical and intra-/inter-institutional dimensions and its impact on effectiveness is subsequently analysed. Finally, chapter 8 looks at the 2015 ENP Review through the prism of this literature review.

---

[4] See Consultation: "Towards a new European Neighbourhood Policy" (http://ec.europa.eu/enlargement/neighbourhood/consultation/list_of_contributions_received.pdf).

2. CONDITIONALITY AND SOCIALISATION

Since 2011 a significant share of the ENP literature has focused on the EU's capacity and determination to achieve its policy objectives in the neighbourhood. The objectives stressed by the literature include democracy, respect for human rights and such fundamental freedoms as freedom of the press and assembly. Among the selected independent variables, conditionality is the single most-stressed factor accounting for the effectiveness of the ENP in the literature dealing particularly with democracy and human rights.

Conditionality may take both a negative and a positive shape, and links the EU's demands (e.g. political reform) with the incentives it offers (e.g. market access or macro-financial assistance). Comelli (2013) argues that the more the EU focuses on implementing positive and negative conditionality, which requires an increased level of differentiation, the greater the degree of fragmentation will be among the countries in the southern neighbourhood. Whereas positive conditionality can only be used in the cases of countries that have successfully gone through the 'Arab Spring' and have started a process of democratic transition, the EU is either "unable or unwilling" to apply negative conditionality.

While conditionality follows the *logic of consequentiality*, socialisation is based on the *logic of appropriateness*. In other words, socialisation is a process through which the partners internalise EU values and norms through conviction and not coercion.

In promoting democracy in the neighbourhood, the EU uses linkages, leverage and functional cooperation with the neighbouring countries' administrations. 'Linkage', defined as bottom-up support for democratic forces, has not produced notable results in the neighbourhood. The linkage model is likely to be successful if there is substantial support for civil society and the modernisation of a targeted country. Moreover, the targeted country should not be isolated and the pro-democratic civil society should be autonomous and have room for manoeuvre (Lavenex and Schimmelfennig, 2011). Sasse (2013) challenges the overwhelming emphasis of the literature on the linkages of Eastern Partnership states with the EU and the US, ignoring their ties to Russia. She explores the relationship between linkages, 'stateness' and democratisation, concluding that "where linkages are not diverse (or where they are framed as being less diverse than they are) and domestic political competition is weak, Western 'democracy promotion' rhetoric and aid are not only ineffective, but also counterproductive" (580-581).

Applying 'leverage' as a top-down approach to sway political elites through conditionality is not without limits, as it is largely linked to an EU membership prospect (as discussed below). The leverage is effective in cases when the tangible (material and political) and intangible (social or symbolic) benefits received from the EU exceed the domestic adoption costs for the targeted country. Not only the effectiveness but also the credibility of the leverage is based on clear and well-defined conditions (Lavenex and Schimmelfennig, 2011). However, the analysis of the ENP action plans with Jordan and Tunisia demonstrates that they contain unclear, random and incoherent benchmarks, which negatively affect the credibility of the EU's conditionality (Del Sarto and Schumacher, 2011). On the other hand, such discrepancies in the action plans could be partially blamed on the fact that the priorities of the ENP action plans are decided through co-ownership by the EU and the neighbouring country. Yet, it is also the result of the absence of determination by the EU (Del Sarto and Schumacher, 2011). Even after the Arab Spring in 2011, a distinct lack of political will by EU member states has hampered the leveraging of the EU's values. The effort to transplant EU values into authoritarian environments through socialisation with North African regimes has not been successful either (Thépaut, 2011).

Morillas (2015: 33) explored the interaction between the EU's conditionality and its ability to act as an external mediator. The case of Egypt illustrates that the balance between the two is difficult as "it has been problematic to pursue a strategy of political dialogue with all parties, not to remove the EU's assistance when the political dialogue fails and still remain a powerful and influential external actor, all at the same time".

Furthermore, some researchers argue that the EU does not pursue coherent democracy promotion and gives more importance to its geostrategic interests. For example, Börzel and Van Hüllen (2014) looked into the action plans concluded between the EU and ENP states. Based on a comparison of provisions on more democratic and more effective governance in ten action plans, the researchers found that "there is a clear imbalance between the extent to which the [action plans] dwell on issues of democratic as opposed to effective governance in favour of provisions on a narrower, technical definition of 'good' governance as the efficiency of state institutions that does not reflect the Commission's initial proposals" (Börzel and Van Hüllen, 2014: 1037). In addition, this emphasis on effective governance is prevalent in such fields as regional security, economic reforms for compliance with European common market rules, domestic security and cooperation on justice and home affairs (border control, migration, organised crime, trafficking, money laundering and corruption). The issue of coherence in the EU's policies vis-à-vis the ENP countries, including coherence in the application of conditionality, is extensively discussed in chapter 7 of this report.

In sum, the EU's conditionality has primarily been directed at the democratisation of the neighbourhood, as democracy is viewed as a necessary component for greater security, stability and prosperity. As opposed to conditionality, socialisation is not based on conditional demands or coercion but on persuasion. The literature is critical of the effectiveness of both conditionality and socialisation in the framework of the ENP.

2.1 Positive conditionality: Membership prospects and visa liberalisation

The development of the concept of conditionality in the context of the ENP is inextricably linked to the enlargement process, especially the EU's experience from its biggest expansion round in 2004 (Buscaneanu, 2012; Cadier, 2013). The absence of the 'golden carrot' of a membership prospect for ENP countries has been said to significantly weaken the application of the principle of conditionality to the neighbourhood countries and undermine the strength of the mutual relationship. A survey conducted by Dostál et al. (2015) among various stakeholders from the countries of the EaP clearly shows that the lack of a membership prospect constitutes a prominent point of concern for many, albeit to varying degrees in different countries. Nevertheless, 91.1% of the survey participants expressed a desire to see membership in the EaP directly connected to EU membership prospects.

Although the ENP in its current design is "modelled on the EU's enlargement policy" with the underlying logic of "attempting to shape the EU's immediate environment by exporting its norms, values and regulations", the ENP cannot be viewed as an alternative to enlargement given the ambiguity the EU included in its initial template, thus creating a setup that allows for enough space for the individual preferences and interests of individual member states (Cadier, 2013: 55). This is relevant especially as the newer EU member states have been significantly more supportive of offering prospective membership to countries in the Eastern 'European' neighbourhood (Cadier, 2013).

The absence of a membership prospect has furthermore affected the legitimacy of the ENP, eroding the expectations of several EaP countries (especially Ukraine, Moldova and Georgia). Other countries, like Belarus and Armenia, have regarded the absence of a membership possibility as proof that the incentives and benefits of the ENP do not outweigh the benefits of a prioritised relationship with the Russian Federation. Nonetheless, several of the EaP countries have undergone reforms, lured by concrete alternative incentives such as visa liberalisation and enhanced association agreements, as well as financial and technical assistance (Börzel and Lebanidze, 2015). When the membership prospect is off the table, EU democracy promotion relies more on the voluntary commitments of the elites of the targeted country to European integration and democratic reforms.

Analysis of Ukraine accepting EU rules demonstrates that although Ukrainian authorities accept a comprehensive list of rules, their adoption and application has been selective. According to Casier (2011), Ukraine's self-imposed conditionality has resulted in progress in terms of formal institutional democracy while falling behind in practising democracy. This asymmetric convergence is characterised by a non-synchronised and highly idiosyncratic approach, leading to a patchy impact of the EU on Ukraine (Langbein and Wolczuk, 2012).

As the literature demonstrates, incentives such as market access or visa dialogue often "are not sizeable enough to pay off the costs of political reforms that undermine the very power base of incumbent regimes as long as they have no genuine interest in Western democracy" (Börzel and Lebanidze, 2015: 12). The benefits offered under the ENP are therefore often vastly outweighed by the domestic costs of the demanded reforms, which are in many cases deeply structural in nature (Cadier, 2013). According to Börzel and Lebanidze (2015), this has been particularly the case for reforms connected to the broader aim of democratisation, such as the reform of state institutions and the rule of law, and less so for several sectoral reforms, for example in the areas of migration, energy and environment.

Ultimately, the effectiveness of EU conditionality fundamentally depends on the cost–benefit calculations made by national and local political elites. That is why the EU's conditionality is also undermined by the interests of oligarchs and their political allies in the area of state aid law in Ukraine (Dimitrova and Dragneva, 2013; Sadowski, 2013). While the strength of external incentives is one part of the equation, the interests of local and domestic elites also ought to be considered. More on this topic is discussed in chapter 4 on ownership and local dynamics.

In the field of justice and home affairs, most studies focus on migration cooperation and mobility (Cassarino, 2014; Eisele and Wiesbrock, 2011; Mananashvili, 2015; Walton-Roberts and Hennebry, 2014). In the absence of a membership prospect, researchers devote attention to the visa liberalisation process, which is considered one of the EU's major transformative instruments, particularly in the eastern neighbourhood (Shapovalova, 2013; Sagrera, 2014; Benedyczak et al., 2015). The EU uses conditionality to incentivise partners to adopt specific policies in exchange for granting visa-free travel to the EU.

Despite the fact that visa liberalisation has been regarded as one of the most consequential instruments of the ENP, Sagrera

(2014) notes that the aim of creating a standardised path towards visa liberalisation is far from being met. Dumas and Lang (2015) observe that migration policy, in particular social security rights, has been more developed with Mediterranean partners, whereas visa liberalisation is more advanced with eastern partners. The authors find that the demand for increased mobility partnerships has accordingly been higher among the neighbourhood countries in the Mediterranean region, and the association agreements with these partners have constituted a "more fruitful framework for cooperation" (Dumas and Lang, 2015).

In dealing with visa liberalisation, the EU's view is predominately informed by security concerns. Yet Shapovalova (2013) points out that visa-free travel is not likely to induce an increased flow of illegal migrants to the EU. It is likely to induce people-to-people contacts and thus promote democratisation and European integration of the EaP countries. It will also boost tourism and encourage trade and business activity.

In 2014, Moldova became only the second neighbourhood country (after Israel) with which a visa liberalisation regime was established. According to Dumas and Lang (2015), the achievement of a successful agreement between Moldova and the EU in this framework has additionally granted the EU credibility and trustworthiness with its partners, showing its commitment to existing agreements against the prioritisation of its interests specifically in the area of border control and management of irregular migration.

In sum, when addressing positive conditionality in the framework of the ENP, the literature concentrates on the lack of membership prospects. Based on the experiences of the 2004 enlargement, the literature argues that the absence of a membership prospect severely limits the effectiveness of the EU's conditionality and thus the transformative power of the EU. In the absence of a membership prospect, visa dialogue becomes one of the most important and tangible incentives for the neighbouring countries. However, given the current environment in the EU, it is unlikely that the southern neighbours will be given a visa liberalisation path anytime soon.

2.2 Negative conditionality

The EU has used negative conditionality against some neighbours in the south and east, implying the imposition of 'punishments' as sanctioning mechanisms for non-compliance with the EU's demands or standards. In analysing the southern neighbourhood, Balfour (2012a: 7-8) challenges the effectiveness of political conditionality in general, arguing that "the focus on political conditionality raises more problems than it solves". According to Balfour (2012a: 17), while "the focus on the mechanics of conditionality obscures the political dynamics and dilemmas that derive from policies which fall more squarely under the category of 'foreign policy', of which the ENP is just one part", the use of political conditionality creates new dilemmas related to engagement with countries that do not reach the desired EU standards and cannot be addressed with the introduction of new benchmarks.

Similarly, Duleba et al. (2012) point out that the increasing emphasis on political as well as normative issues (i.e. 'European values') in the EU's relations with Ukraine have ultimately presented more of an obstacle to strengthening cooperation, especially in terms of bilateral trade relations. Even though this could be seen as positive with respect to policy formulation on the EU's side, the authors argue that this approach could possibly bring more risks than benefits, in case it does not bear any results in terms of improving political relations. A largely normative-based policy formulation may clash with the interests, for example in security or energy, of individual member states. This is further discussed in chapter 3 of this report.

Conversely, Montesano et al. (2016) argue for a strict conditionality vis-à-vis Moldova. They criticise the EU's budget support for Moldova, which is soft on conditionality and is not effective in terms of results. They back the EU's suspension of budget support for Moldova after the 2015 banking fraud, arguing that it should have happened earlier: "Indeed, less strict conditionality on the part of the EU undermines the Moldovan citizens' trust in Brussels, as they associate this with collusion with their corrupt local elites. The fact that Moldovan public support for EU integration actually went up after the suspension of payments provides a striking illustration of this point" (Montesano et al., 2016: 15).

In analysing sanctions imposed on Tunisia (on 48 individuals), Egypt (on 19 individuals), Libya and Syria following the Arab revolutions, Giumelli (2011) suggests that they follow the coercing-constraining-signalling approach rather than the behavioural change logic. Their goal has been to undermine those under the sanctions and support the transition process. In Tunisia and Egypt, the sanctions targeted the families and associates of former presidents. In Libya the EU sanctions were aimed at isolating Muammar Gaddafi and supporting transition. In Syria, EU sanctions aimed at persuading President Bashar al-Assad to negotiate with the rebels and the international community. After the failure of this approach, the sanctions were used for changing and constraining the regime. In analysing the EU's sanctions against Syria, Portela (2012) finds that the EU has put in place sophisticated sanctions that have visible economic effects despite the fact that they were undermined by Russian action. These sanctions, however, were not suited to stopping the bloodshed.

Would alternative actions deliver better results than sanctions? Giumelli (2013: 35) argues that

> [i]n the absence of sanctions, Assad may have had a greater incentive to limit the use of force to preserve his legitimacy in the eyes of the international community, but in fact he began to use violence when sanctions were not in place. Moreover, their lifting at this point of the crisis would serve to legitimise Assad's behaviour rather than condemn it.

In general, as the EU and the US encouraged revolts in the southern Mediterranean, they have taken on an obligation to support those standing against the regimes. Not doing so would send a negative message affecting their image and undermine their support of democratic principles.

Through the application of historical institutionalism, Boogaerts et al. (2016) investigate whether the Arab Spring represents a critical juncture for the EU's policy towards the southern Mediterranean. By analysing Egypt, Libya, Syria and Tunisia, the authors conclude that only the EU's sanctions vis-à-vis Syria constitute a turning point in the EU's use of this instrument.

In comparison, the sanctions imposed against Syria were heavy and implemented in a very short period of time. In general, the EU does not have the necessary processes in place to react to sudden revolutions, which explains its slow and cautious approach.

The effectiveness of the negative conditionality is also questioned in relation to the Transnistrian conflict (Giumelli, 2013). The EU used travel bans against political elites in the Transnistrian region, which were first introduced in 2003 within the framework of the EU's external action in Moldova and aimed at helping to resolve the Transnistrian conflict. On the one hand, in combination with other instruments that were implemented in the region, the use of travel bans has led to the isolation of certain actors, limiting their capabilities and undermining their legitimacy. This has contributed to the EU's strategy in the region. On the other hand, the research also reveals several missteps and increased risks attached to the EU's strategy.

> [T]here is a widespread view that the EU has designed the resolution of sanctions in a rush, without allowing itself an 'exit strategy' for lifting the ban. This created a game of chicken situation, which should have been avoided. Another common criticism regards the reshuffling that took place in February 2008, when aside from the name of Evgeny Shevchuk, the other five names that were added resembled more the need of maintaining a constant number of people in the list rather than a reasoned decision to target the responsible for the stalemate in the negotiation. There is also a prevalent belief that sanctions are not helping but instead are damaging the overall conflict resolution strategy of the international community (Giumelli, 2011, 374-375).

In sum, despite the difficulty of detecting the extent to which the imposition of travel bans has been actively contributing to conflict resolution, their lifting would weaken the EU's role in the region and the effectiveness of the overall strategy.

Analysing the EU's 2008-10 sanctions against Belarus and their subsequent easing, Portela (2012) concludes that the impact of the sanctions on rapprochement with Belarus was minimal. The accommodation by Belarus of the EU's demands was mainly due to the envisaged economic benefits from improved cooperation with the EU.

Moreover, the EU was selective and inconsistent in applying conditionality (Lehne, 2014). For example, according to Grant (2011: 13),

> the EU has a strategic interest in persuading Azerbaijan to support the Nabucco pipeline project, and to sell Europeans gas, but if the EU lets values be the main guide of its relations with autocratic Azerbaijan, it would spurn close ties. Those strategic interests help to explain why the EU has been tougher on Belarus than Azerbaijan – despite there being more political prisoners in Baku than in Minsk.

As Raik notes, the EU did not alter its policies towards Azerbaijan, including the then ongoing negotiations on an action plan (concluded in 2006), in spite of electoral fraud during the 2005 elections and a violent crackdown of the protest that followed (Raik, 2012: 568). Thus, the EU opted not to undermine its relations with an important regional and energy partner, yet at the same time, used a wide spectrum of negative conditionality towards a state where the EU's interest was minimal. But the EU has been more ambitious in promoting its values vis-à-vis the eastern neighbourhood than to southern neighbours.

The literature analyses the scope and effectiveness of sanctions introduced by the EU as a reaction to the illegal annexation of Crimea by Russia and its involvement in the military conflict in the Eastern Ukraine (Raik et al., 2014; Connolly, 2015; Johnston, 2015; Dolidze, 2015; Bond et al., 2015; Ćwiek-Karpowicz and Secrieru, 2015). More specifically, there have been several attempts to investigate the real impact of the EU's sanctions and Russian counter-sanctions on the Russian and European economies (Gros and Mustilli, 2015; Dreger et al., 2016).

According to Gros and Mustilli (2015: 1), the fact that the EU focused on using economic sanctions as the primary instrument in reaction to the annexation of Crimea demonstrates that "the EU's foreign policy instruments are limited to soft power". Nevertheless, according to some authors, sanctions "have so far been the most effective instrument of Western influence on Russia's policy towards Ukraine" (Ćwiek-Karpowicz and Secrieru, 2015: 7).

The literature additionally mentions a so-called boomerang effect of the sanctions (Dolidze, 2015: 1). Although economic sanctions have significantly affected the Russian economy, it is not clear how much the 'countermeasures' introduced by Russia have affected other countries' economies in the region (Gros and Mustilli, 2015; Dreger et al., 2016). Furthermore, while the sanctions are likely to be effective in economic terms, Connolly (2015: 2) argues that "the longer EU and US sanctions persist, the more the market-oriented policy elite is likely to be marginalized as economic policies consistent with a more statist and introverted approach take hold". Although the sanctions have aimed at reversing Russian policies in the eastern neighbourhood, according to Ćwiek-Karpowicz and Secrieru (2015), sanctions are perceived merely as an attempt to undermine the Russian regime and bring about domestic political change. Building on the dynamics in domestic politics in Russia, Bond et al. (2015) argue that the sanctions could ultimately cause a continuation of the existing nature of Russian foreign policy. Furthermore, as chapter 7 illustrates in more detail, there has been a significant level of incoherence in the structuring and implementation of the sanctions, thus limiting their effect.

According to Dreger et al. (2016), another important consideration is how the conflict in Ukraine, in which developments point more and more towards a 'frozen conflict', is going to affect the Ukrainian economy, given its high dependency on Russia. As a result of the conflict and the boomerang effect of the sanctions, both the Ukrainian and Russian economies could suffer significant deterioration in the long term (Dreger et al., 2016). Still, some authors are supportive of a long-term continuation or imposition of tougher sanctions on Russia in reaction to the crisis in Ukraine (Bond et al., 2015; Ćwiek-Karpowicz and Secrieru, 2015).

In sum, the literature about negative conditionality gives much attention to the suspension of the EU's aid and especially sanctions. Scholars debate sanctions against neighbours such as Syria, Libya, Tunisia, Egypt and Belarus. Some scholars also point out the double standards when applying sanctions (e.g. Belarus vs Azerbaijan). Both the purpose of sanctions and their effectiveness vis-à-vis the ENP countries are the subject of debates. Beyond the ENP, economic sanctions have also constituted one of the primary policy instruments deployed by the EU in response to the assertive nature of Russian intervention in Ukraine. While the literature argues that it is pivotal to maintain sanctions against Russia, there is little analysis on the possible backlash that the sanctions create against the EU or their effects on the ENP countries. Chapter 6 of this report addresses the topic of Russian influence on the effectiveness of the EU's policies in the eastern neighbourhood in more detail.

2.3   Conditionality in the 2011 and 2015 ENP Reviews: More for more and differentiation

The EU's response to the Arab Spring by issuing on 25 May 2011 the "New Response to a Changing Neighbourhood" formed the basis of the 2011 ENP Review, highlighting ideas such as the '3Ms' (markets, money and mobility) and 'more for more' as positive conditionality, and 'less for less' as negative conditionality. Achieving 'deep democracy' was proclaimed as the goal of the revised ENP.

A central element of the 2011 ENP Review, namely "more-for-more" and "less-for-less" conditionality, has been subject to a lot of academic debate (Lannon, 2015) despite the fact that the logic of the principle was not new and was part of the inception of the ENP (Van Hüllen, 2012). Initially, the EU viewed the Arab Spring as a window of opportunity for democracy promotion and political change (Dandashly, 2015). According to Bicchi (2014), there are some changes in the way the EU assists democracy in the region: for example, the EU has started to use a more differentiated approach. Nevertheless, as Bicchi shows with the example of the European Instrument for Democracy and Human Rights II (EIDHR II), the EU continues to give preference to the promotion of human rights (those of women and children, for instance) over the promotion of democracy per se (Bicchi, 2014). Analysing the implementation of the post-Arab Spring less-for-less and more-for-more variants of the Union's conditionality strategy in the southern neighbourhood, Bicchi (2014) finds that although there has been an increase in institutional actors and, to some extent, more financial assistance available, the amount of funds that have been disbursed to Arab countries in the Mediterranean has actually decreased, while the policy has remained unchanged.

An important obstacle to the effectiveness of the more-for-more principle is the consistency of its application: "The EU was consistent in deploying the ENP only in regard to Georgia and Ukraine rewarding their relative performance with increased material benefits, compared to those provided before 2004. In the rest of cases the EU has provided increased benefits under the ENP in the absence of sustained or any democratic progress" (Buscaneanu, 2012: 36). This is particularly relevant for the use of political conditionality. The EU has been criticised for leveraging inconsistently with the different countries of the ENP, applying differentiation based solely on its own interests – as demonstrated by the case of oil-rich Azerbaijan, against which the EU has hardly invoked political conditionality owing to its energy interests in the region. Despite Azerbaijan's lack of progress in achieving the political benchmarks attached to ENP conditionality, such as respect for human rights and rule of law, EU-Azerbaijan relations in the areas of trade and energy have rather been strengthened. Analysing the eastern neighbourhood, Hale (2012) concludes that the more-for-more and less-for-less approach is not sufficient to influence autocratic regimes in countries such as Azerbaijan and recommends adding a 'more-for-less' principle. She argues that the EU has leverage vis-à-vis Azerbaijan, and should utilise it for the sake of incorporating human rights in the relationship.

Going beyond the more-for-more principle, a volume edited by Bouris and Schumacher (2016) provides an in-depth analysis of the 2011 revision of the ENP through the prism of continuity and change. The volume addresses markers and types of changes in the neighbourhood and the EU's response to them as well as the changes in the EU's revised institutional architecture. A central point is to identify the effects of both internal and external changes brought about by the 2011 ENP Review.

Through application of post-structuralism, Cebeci (2016) argues that despite slight changes of discourse in the 2011 revised ENP – especially related to civil society – the EU continued to present itself as an 'ideal power Europe' through which it legitimised imposing its longstanding practice of governmentality on the neighbours. Yet, when faced with difficult realities that test the EU's ability to attain the goals of the ENP, the EU's hegemonic claim became less normative than it was prior to the 2011 ENP Review (Haukkala, 2016).

Whether or not the 2011 Review constituted a change is also challenged by legal scholars. The legal framework of the ENP is "path dependant" to past experiences, with some spillover effects from other EU policies (Van Elsuwege and Van der Loo, 2016). Despite the inclusion of Art. 8 in the Treaty on European Union (TEU), the EU continues to give preference to bilateral relations with the neighbours through association agreements (including deep and comprehensive trade areas, DCFTAs), as well as mobility, migration, energy and aviation agreements. Moreover, the enactment of the Lisbon Treaty and establishment of the EEAS did not change considerably the institutional equilibrium of the EU as far the implementation of the 2011 revised ENP is concerned (Kostanyan, 2016a). By contrast, the European Parliament managed to carve out a greater role for itself in the revised ENP through the use of formal and informal means (Kaminska, 2016).

To a lesser extent the literature addresses the effects of the 2011 revised ENP on EU policy towards the unresolved conflicts. In analysing the conflicts in the South Caucasus, Freizer (2016) finds that the Review consolidated the toolbox of the ENP, including the Common Foreign and Security Policy (CFSP) and communitarian elements. From a social-constructivist perspective, Natorski (2016) argues that following the 2011 ENP Review there is a continuity of the EU's reformist agenda vis-à-vis Ukraine "along with its 'change by addition' of Russia to the framework of EU-Ukraine debates during the crisis and war in Ukraine" (Natorski, 2016: 191). The major issues related to the EU-centred technocratic approach to the Israeli–Palestinian conflict was not altered by the 2011 Review either (Müller, 2016).

An important dilemma for the EU has been to choose between one-size-fits-all approaches and differentiating policies long before the recent 2015 Review of the ENP. More differentiated policies can become especially complex as there are no clear criteria for conditionality. The lack of clear definitions of benchmarks and crucial terms (such as 'democracy') that are at the centre of the EU's use of conditionality significantly hinders both the credibility and attractiveness of the EU's policies. Analysis of the ENP action plans with Jordan and Tunisia demonstrate that the benchmarks are unclear, arbitrary and incoherent, which harms the credibility of conditionality (Del Sarto and Schumacher, 2011). In the wake of the Arab Spring, the calls for the EU to clarify benchmarks for sanctions and rewards in the EU's democracy promotion have intensified and been linked to its effectiveness and credibility. Moreover, the implementation of differentiation requires clear strategic guidelines. In addition to political dialogue, assistance, association councils and subcommittees for the cooperation, the EU has to support civil society in a more coordinated fashion (Van Hüllen, 2012).

In fact, the stress on differentiation in the 2015 Review of the ENP is a result of accepting reality in the neighbourhood and is an attempt to incorporate diverse needs and desires of the partners. This is particularly apparent for the partners that are unwilling or unable to accept the association agreements and the DCFTAs with the EU. The new ENP "goes further by assuming that neighbouring regions and countries do not constitute a unified geographical, political and economic space. This is because in recent years, developments in both the eastern and southern neighbourhoods have blatantly exposed the baffling discrepancies between partners' responses to the EU" (Delcour, 2016b: 295).

Differentiation is also applied in the Commission's regular reporting on progress (or regress) made by the neighbours. The new ENP abandons the enlargement-style reporting in favour of shorter and more political assessments. According to Delcour (2016b: 294-295), the Review implicitly accepts that the enlargement-style conditionality did not deliver the anticipated results in domestic reforms in the neighbourhood countries.

In sum, the emerging academic literature is critical of the 2011 ENP Review and even more so of its implementation. (The 2015 ENP Review is discussed in the final chapter of this report.) Despite the Arab revolts and the changes in the EU's institutional architecture as a result of the enactment of the Treaty of Lisbon, scholars often observe continuation in how the EU deals with its neighbours rather than change. Tömmel's (2013: 36) findings are sobering in this respect: "the EU did not adequately exploit this opportunity, neither for overcoming its internal constraints nor for providing effective assistance to the partner states on their thorny path towards democratic reform". This outcome is not surprising, as the EU's actions were constrained by interactions between the Commission and the member states in the Council, as well as by the tensions between the EU's normative aspirations and realist interests. In this context the expectations and needs of the neighbours have not been prioritised.

2.4 Sectoral cooperation

Going beyond linkage and leverage, Lavenex and Schimmelfennig (2011: 885) propose the so-called governance model of democracy promotion, which "does not tackle the core institutions of the political system as such, but promotes transparency, accountability, and participation at the level of state administration". This functional approach hinges on approximation of the neighbourhood countries to EU norms and rules in a whole host of sectors through cooperation between the EU and public administrations of the targeted countries.

The EU has entered into considerable sectoral and economic cooperation with neighbouring countries. Freyburg et al. (2011) compare competition, environmental and migration policies in Jordan and Morocco in the southern neighbourhood, and Moldova and Ukraine in the eastern neighbourhood. The findings demonstrate that the degree of political liberalisation and membership aspiration do not explain the variation in democracy promotion in Jordan and Morocco, on the one hand, and Moldova and Ukraine, on the other hand. In all selected countries there is a clear discrepancy between the adoption of a rule and its application. Freyburg et al. (2011) hypothesise that in fact sectoral cooperation is the precondition to democratic governance. However, sectoral cooperation as an avenue for democracy promotion is effective under certain conditions, namely when the EU *acquis* is incorporated in the legislation of the targeted country; when there is an institutionalised relationship between the EU and the neighbour, whose administration is autonomous; and when the adoption costs of the reforms are not high.

The analysis of economic relations looks at the neighbourhood in general (Astrov et al., 2012) as well as the southern (Gligorov et al., 2012) and eastern (Adarov et al., 2015; Havlik, 2014) dimensions in particular. Since the EU started to negotiate and conclude association agreements and DCFTAs with some of its ENP partners, several publications have analysed the scope and contents of these ambitious deals.

Whereas some contributions examine the negotiation process (Kostanyan, 2014a), the scope and contents of the DCFTAs with the Mediterranean (Pieters, 2013; Lannon, 2014) or eastern ENP countries (Van der Loo, 2016a; Emerson et al., 2016a, 2016b, 2016c), other publications analyse how and to what extent these (envisaged) DCFTAs promote the EU's *acquis* to the ENP countries (Van der Loo, 2014, 2016b; Van Elsuwege and Petrov, 2014). In addition, Manoli (2013) explores the political economy aspects of the DCFTAs. In support of DCFTA negotiations, DG Trade commissioned from Ecorys and CASE (2012) a trade sustainability impact assessment of relevant neighbouring countries.

CEPS contributed to the analysis of the association agreements and DCFTAs through a trilogy of handbooks on Ukraine (Emerson et al., 2016a), Moldova (Emerson et al., 2016b) and Georgia (Emerson et al., 2016c). The books adopt a fairly neutral approach, starting with an explanation of the commitments entered into by the contracting parties in the agreements, and followed by analysis of the realities on the ground and the progress made by each of the three neighbours. The agreement covers political alignment, economic integration and sectoral cooperation with the EU. The political goal of the association agreements is to fulfil the European aspirations and choices of the associated countries through realising democracy, human rights and the rule of law. The DCFTAs and sectoral cooperation chapters go beyond eliminating tariffs and quantitative restrictions, and include provisions geared towards legal harmonisation and supporting the modernisation of the associated countries' economies, boosting trade and improving conditions for investment. The books find that the agreements do not provide a 'magic wand' to cure the economic and political problems of Georgia, Moldova and Ukraine in the short term. The agreements are rather roadmaps for development and modernisation of the signatory states and are expected to have effects in the long term.

Many of the studies analysing sectoral cooperation between the EU and the ENP countries focus on cooperation in the area of energy, in particular the Energy Community Treaty (Petrov, 2012;

Filippos, 2016; Buschle, 2014) and aviation (Charokopos, 2013). Blockmans and Van Vooren (2012) explore the benefits of "legally binding sectoral multilateralism", i.e. a treaty-based legal integration between the EU and neighbouring countries and between the latter themselves, in sectors where this is clearly beneficial in its own right, e.g. transport, energy and migration. The authors consider that the vehicle of binding sectoral multilateralism offers promising prospects for the extension of the EU's legal order in the neighbourhood, as long as it is approached in a functional manner.

The attempt to export EU law to the neighbourhood countries is apparent particularly in the energy sector through both multilateral (e.g. the Energy Community) and bilateral agreements (e.g. association agreements). Buschle (2014) argues that such 'juridification' of external policy is preferable to diplomatic relations. Still, the point is rather theoretical at this stage. Harpaz (2014) challenges the transformative role of the law as being limited by the ENP's weak negative conditionality and uncharitable incentives. Instead the author recommends that the EU give attention to establishing "enhanced cooperative ties and closer institutional linkages that may better succeed in advancing, on an ad hoc basis, trade-related, less politicized, policy/sector basis regulatory and legislative alignment" (Harpaz, 2014: 451). In evaluating the EU's promotion of environmental policy in Morocco, Maggi (2012) points out the need for capacity building in order to make the implementation of the policy possible. She argues that the cross-sectoral nature of environmental policy should be factored in by the EU.

In sum, there are discrepancies concerning how the scholars view the nature and the purpose of sectoral cooperation between the EU and the neighbourhood countries. Some studies argue that sectoral cooperation is an avenue for democratisation. Others see it as a tool to reform specific policy areas. The link between reforms through sectoral cooperation and democratisation, although theoretically possible, requires further empirical research.

2.5 Institutionalisation of the ENP

The literature also examines different forms of institutionalisation of the ENP through which the EU aims to transfer its norms and values to the neighbouring countries, including issuing annual country reports (a practice that was abandoned with the 2015 ENP Review). Besides intergovernmental bilateral and multilateral tracks of the ENP (Kostanyan and Orbie, 2013), scholars consider the functioning of multilateral parliamentary cooperation (EuroNest) within the EaP (Kostanyan and Vandecasteele, 2013; Petrova and Raube, 2016) and the Civil Society Forum (Kostanyan, 2014b; Shapovalova, 2015).

As opposed to bilateral relations that include legally binding commitments for the partners, the multilateral frameworks of the ENP are rather political in nature and provide a platform for an exchange of views and best practices (Kostanyan and Orbie, 2013). Therefore, the intergovernmental frameworks with their ministerial meetings, thematic platforms of officials or panels of experts operating under the ENP are not fit for the application of a strong form of conditionality.

Similarly, conditionality is not at the centre of the multilateral EU–Eastern Partnership Parliamentary Assembly (EuroNest PA), which is characterised by institutionalisation, socialisation and diplomacy (Petrova and Raube, 2016). EuroNest managed to organise a number of meetings and issue several declaratory resolutions but did not succeed in inducing political and economic integration through cooperation between the European and the EaP countries' parliaments. The parliamentarians from the EaP countries in particular have primarily addressed bilateral issues rather than engaged in multilateral cooperation. Moreover, the use of negative conditionality by excluding Belarus (citing lack of free and fair elections) while welcoming Azerbaijan into the assembly was criticised as a double standard by the EU (Kostanyan and Vandecasteele, 2015).

Besides working with the governments of the neighbourhood countries on bilateral and multilateral levels, the EU has also engaged with the civil societies of partner countries. Similar to the intergovernmental and parliamentary dimensions of the ENP, the EU's cooperation with civil society operating in the neighbourhood has also been highly institutionalised and chiefly concerned with non-government organisations. Some authors have argued for broadening the definition of civil society by including trade unions and business associations (Falkenhain and Solonenko, 2012).

Although civil society had been brought to the forefront of the EU's Mediterranean and EaP policies following the events of the Arab Spring, little has been done to develop a clear strategy on cooperation with civil society organisations despite their portrayal as key cooperation partners in the EU's official communications and policy documents. According to Boiten (2015), the EU's conceptualisation of civil society as a "force for political liberalisation" effectively limits EU support for civil society organisations. Whereas civil society actors conceptualise democracy and their own role as a pathway to sustainable development, economic welfare and so forth, the EU's view is limited to that of political liberalisation and achievement of democracy. Falkenhain and Solonenko (2012) advocate a stronger role for civil society as a reform ally in the EU's relations with the eastern partners. They argue that it will result in a greater impact as civil society may pressure governments to reform.

In 2009 the EU institutionalised the Eastern Partnership Civil Society Forum. The Forum has its own secretariat, steering committee, working groups and national platforms that have facilitated a socialisation process among participants (Kostanyan, 2014b). But the Civil Society Forum's advocacy potential is underused and its brand is underappreciated (Shapovalova, 2015).

In direct support of civil society in the neighbouring countries, the EU has established the European Endowment for Democracy through which the EU institutions and some member states provide assistance to civil society that is not able to benefit from the EU's support otherwise (Kostanyan and Nasieniak, 2012). The European Endowment for Democracy has been a valuable addition to civil society support. Yet, according to Youngs (2015), it

> still needs to find ways of locating genuinely new democracy activists. It must devise tactics capable of neutering regimes' attacks on its projects. It needs to develop techniques for monitoring the impact of its civil society support beyond the short term. And it still has to

draw together its assortment of individual projects into a more comprehensive model of political change.

In addressing the southern neighbourhood, Dennison and Dworkin (2011) argue that in the post-Arab revolt period the EU should support the creation of an inclusive political environment through assisting the development of legitimate and accountable governments without backing any particular political entity. This should also be a guiding principle for the European Endowment for Democracy if EU conditionality is to be effective.

In a nutshell, the EU has institutionalised its relations with the ENP countries through bilateral and multilateral fora. Besides the intergovernmental level, the EU also cooperates with its neighbours through a multilateral parliamentary assembly and civil society forum. The European Endowment for Democracy is the latest innovative addition to the set of institutions dealing with the neighbourhood. Whereas in the bilateral intergovernmental formats the EU uses both conditionality and socialisation, the multilateral tracks mainly serve as a platform for socialisation.

2.6 Conclusion

Conditionality and socialisation are addressed exhaustively by the literature in relation to the effectiveness of the ENP. They are particularly dealt with by scholars in the context of EU democracy support to the neighbourhood. The conditionality literature centres on the attractiveness, clarity and credibility of the EU's offer, the determination of the EU in the implementation phase and the result of the EU's leverage vis-à-vis the neighbourhood countries. The conditionality literature is rather negative about the effectiveness of the ENP in achieving democracy in the neighbourhood.

Negative conditions and positive incentives tied to the EU's assistance, and institutionalised cooperation with the neighbours in different dimensions are addressed in the context of conditionality. The literature treats the membership prospect as the most attractive instrument in democracy promotion. The lack of a membership prospect in the ENP weakens its attractiveness and thus the effectiveness of the EU's conditionality.

In the absence of a membership prospect, the EU has offered visa dialogue, financial and technical assistance, and economic and sectoral cooperation. Visa facilitation or liberalisation bring about tangible results in the framework of the ENP. In 2014 Moldova became only the second neighbourhood country (after Israel) with which a visa liberalisation regime was established. The achievement of a successful agreement between Moldova and the EU in this framework has additionally granted the EU credibility and trustworthiness with its partners, showing its commitment to existing agreements against the prioritisation of its interests specifically in the area of border control and management of irregular migration (Dumas and Lang, 2015). However, this has been followed by complications in the same process for Georgia and Ukraine. And as far as the southern neighbourhood is concerned, the offer of visa liberalisation is not even on the political agenda.

A majority of scholars argue that the EU's offer (i.e. incentives) is not sizeable enough to offset the costs of domestic change in the ENP countries. Eventually, the effectiveness of conditionality is to a considerable degree determined by cost–benefit analyses by the governments of partner countries. The more-for-more and less-for-less principles stressed by the 2011 Review did not constitute a substantial change in EU policy vis-à-vis the neighbourhood.

The use of negative conditionality, such as sanctions or freezing EU support to those countries suffering from democratic deficits or highly corrupt regimes, is the subject of debate in many publications. Our review shows that there is no consensus on the use of negative measures. Some scholars argue that the EU's conditionality will be stronger if there are stricter sanctions against those violating the EU's values; others view sanctions as counterproductive.

The EU not only uses leverage but also creates linkages and sectoral cooperation with the neighbouring countries. To varying degrees, the EU is engaged in a wide range of economic and sectoral cooperation with its neighbourhood countries. Yet, the effects of this cooperation on the democratisation of neighbourhood countries have been limited. And in general terms, the link between sectoral cooperation and democracy promotion requires further empirical research.

To sum up, with some exceptions, many of the scholars argue for stronger conditionality vis-à-vis neighbours. Nevertheless, the overwhelming majority of the authors conclude that, thus far, the application of ENP conditionality has not achieved the expected results. The underlying assumption is that the conditionality does not work because its design and implementation are flawed. Two major gaps can be identified from the literature. First, democracy promotion is the major purpose of the conditionality, but there are cases where the EU imposes conditionality vis-à-vis the neighbours in trade and many aspects of sectoral cooperation. A second limitation stems from the fact that it often gives immense weight to the EU's leverage and overlooks other factors (e.g. local conditions and receptiveness, non-EU (f)actors) relevant to the effectiveness of the ENP.

3. INTERESTS VS. VALUES

3.1 The ambiguous nature of values

There is consensus in the literature that when facing an interests-vs-values dilemma, the EU prioritises the former. This is in spite of the fact that the promotion of values is strengthened by the Treaty of Lisbon in Art. 8 TEU (Hillion, 2013). Moreover, according to Gstöhl (2016b), the role of EU values in its external actions is highly contested because of the ambiguity of values and potential conflict between them. While the definition of norms and values – which also comprise social norms about appropriate behaviour – is not solely limited to legal frameworks, researchers argue that it is important first to evaluate how values, given their symbolic significance for the EU, found practical expression in the EU's legal order and Treaties (Cremona, 2011: 275; Gstöhl, 2016b). In particular, it is crucial to trace how the EU's normative identity has been extended to the ENP goals.

In general terms, scholars distinguish between two types of foreign policy objectives pursued by a nation state, which can also be applied to the EU: possession goals and milieu goals (Ghazaryan, 2014; Nielsen and Vilson, 2014). The latter ones deal with the transformation of an actor's external environment while trying to combine altruism and self-interest. In this regard, the ENP pursues its set of milieu goals, which include the promotion of democracy, human rights and the rule of law, respect of international law, conflict resolution, environmental protection and good neighbourly relations (Ghazaryan, 2014: 13). By contrast, the possession goals, which can be also defined as strategic objectives, concern themselves with the narrower interests of the EU in economics and trade, migration, border management, energy security and conflict resolution (Nielsen and Vilson, 2014: 235).

In her study on democracy promotion as a milieu goal of the EU, Ghazaryan (2014) shows that during the pre-Lisbon period the

EU defined its 'founding' principles (Art. 6 of the Amsterdam Treaty) to include democracy, liberty, respect for human rights and fundamental freedoms, and the rule of law. At the same time, democracy promotion as an external objective of the EU was given a rather general character, though it was "mainstreamed, since political dialogue and 'essential' clauses have become common practice in the conclusion of international agreements" (Ghazaryan, 2014: 14-15). The Lisbon Treaty confirmed the EU's mandate to promote democracy abroad, but the Treaty did so in a rather confusing way due to the different wordings used in its articles.

First, in the Lisbon Treaty the concepts of 'principle' and 'value' are used interchangeably: democracy features in EU external relations as a value, as a principle and as an objective (Art. 21 TEU and Art. 205 of the Treaty on the Functioning of the European Union (TFEU)) (Ghazaryan, 2014: 17). Nonetheless, these concepts should be distinguished as they entail different ideas. While values stand for internal, ethical beliefs and guidelines, principles are characterised as legal norms that put limitations on the EU's actions: compliance with principles, in contrast to values, is strictly obligatory. As Von Bogdandy argues, the use of 'value' instead of a 'principle' demonstrates a present lack of determination as regards the founding EU principles (Von Bogdandy, 2010: 22, cited in Ghazaryan, 2014: 17). Furthermore, one should distinguish between principles and objectives: the latter serves as an indicator for the final aim of the action (Von Bogdandy, 2010: 23). Therefore, as Ghazaryan states, "the external actions of the EU are limited by the principle of democracy by which it has to be 'guided', at the same time attempting to achieve consolidation of democracy as an end goal of its international efforts" (Ghazaryan, 2014: 17).

Second, the EU's objectives are not balanced, and the priority is given to the CFSP (Dashwood et al., 2011: 904-905). The objectives are formulated broadly to reflect the EU's interests in international security, economic development, multilateral cooperation and other areas. This in turn creates a legal space for the EU to pursue both possession and milieu goals: to be a rational and a normative actor, depending on the circumstances. Prioritising objectives related to the CFSP (which has an intergovernmental nature) can lead to "securitisation" of the majority of external action areas, and allow the member states to pursue their own interests detached from the normative agenda of the EU (Ghazaryan, 2014: 18). As Lehne argues, "for reasons linked to the notion of European identity, the EU as such gives prominence to governance and human rights issues in its embryonic foreign policy. This leaves Member States free to pursue policies based on their own particular interests" (Lehne, 2014: 221).

Nonetheless, democracy promotion is considered a general obligation for the EU and its members: Arts 3(5) and 21(1) TEU point out that promotion of democracy as the EU's value has to be applied to all spheres of the Union's external relations. In addition, the wider interpretation of Art. 49 TEU suggests that democracy promotion is crucial for the EU's identity, particularly because candidate states are required to be "committed" to the promotion of EU values, including democracy.

Still, the inclusion of democracy promotion in the legal basis of the EU's foreign policy goals (and thus affirmation of the EU's normative identity) does not mean that this objective has a priority position among other aims. The principle of 'complementarity' that applies to different external policy areas, as well as a requirement (Art. 3(5) TEU, Art. 21(2)) to safeguard both values and interests, can result in the prioritisation of 'vital' possession goals at the expense of a milieu goal. Also, there is a discrepancy about the milieu goals to be advanced. As Gstöhl (2016b) argues, the EU has tended to prioritise the first generation of human rights, civil and political rights over the second generation of economic, social and cultural rights in its external relations.

At the same time, one should not neglect the socio-economic set of values promoted by the EU along with political ones (Gstöhl, 2016b). The EU Charter of Fundamental Rights, in addition to civil and political rights, includes social and economic rights, while the establishment of an internal market, sustainable development and "a highly competitive social market economy" (Art. 3(3) TEU) are recognised as elements of the EU's aims to promote "the well-being of its people" Art. 3(1) TEU. Notably, solidarity is an explicit goal of EU external action (Art. 21(1) TEU). This set of values also applies to EU relations with the ENP partners, particularly in the process of deep economic integration (DCFTAs), which implies a legal approximation to or adoption of the Union's *acquis*. The 2011 ENP Review introduced the notion of "deep democracy". In addition to free and fair elections, freedom of association and expression, the rule of law and the fight against corruption, the ENP Review also included requirements on security and law-enforcement sector reform and the establishment of democratic control over armed and security forces (European Commission and High Representative, 2011: 3; Gstöhl, 2016b). The association agreements/DCFTAs contain an even larger set of requirements — "common values conditionality" — that go beyond human rights and democratic principles, and include, for example, the principles of free market economy or the promotion of sustainable development and effective multilateralism (Van der Loo et al., 2014: 12). However, Kurki notes that despite introduction of the idea of "deep democracy", there was not any major shift in the EU's conceptual approach towards democracy promotion: the "fuzzily" liberal democratic model remained a main reference point in the EU's rhetoric and documents (Kurki, 2012). Moreover, as Gstöhl (2016b) argues, "economic and political values can be at odds — and the economic concern often prevails": the EU tends to prioritise the establishment of a free market and economic liberalisation over human rights and democratic principles. Potential conflicts could even be found within the same group of values, for example between trade liberalisation on the one hand and sustainable development and poverty reduction on the other (Gstöhl, 2016b; Börzel and van Hüllen, 2014). Based on the aforementioned arguments, Ghazaryan (2014: 20) states that "the Treaty creates a scope for achieving traditional interest-orientated objectives alongside or instead of democracy promotion".

Another major point of criticism of the EU's efforts to promote values is that there is no benchmark that defines the extent to which democracy should be promoted: the EU's legal framework allows a minimal threshold for compliance with the given requirement. For example, the inclusion of an essential elements clause (on democracy or human rights) in a trade agreement with another partner will satisfy the requirement of 'taking account' of the particular objective.

Furthermore, the ambiguity of promoted values may be exacerbated not only by the conflicting norms mentioned in the Treaties, but also by the difference in individual agreements between the EU and ENP states depending on their region. In her other work, Ghazaryan (2016) compares how the EU shapes some of its milieu values (democracy, the rule of law and human rights) when it deals with its eastern and southern neighbours.

First, the researcher explores how the EU values were transferred to the ENP founding documents and action plans before the Arab Spring took place. Ghazaryan argues that, while the 2003 Wider Europe Communication and 2004 ENP Strategy Paper employ the concept of "shared values" and in general do not distinguish between the two regions, some issues are not equally reflected in all action plans. For example, there is a stronger emphasis on women's rights, fighting discrimination, racism and xenophobia in the case of action plans for Egypt, Jordan, Lebanon, Morocco and Tunisia. Moreover, additional actions such as ensuring international justice related to the International Criminal Court were included in the action plans for Ukraine and Moldova. Moreover, while the action plans for the first group of ENP states (the MENA region plus Ukraine and Moldova) were criticised for their general character and poor benchmarking, the action plans for the second group (Armenia, Georgia and Azerbaijan) addressed a limited number of issues and were even more restrictive in their interpretation of EU values. However, there was not an obvious split between the south and the east in the way the EU defined its values (Ghazaryan, 2016: 13-16).

Second, while the Arab Spring has affected the ENP agenda, it has not resulted in a regional split in terms of understanding of the concept of democracy. Instead, the EU has introduced the ideal concept of "deep and sustainable democracy" to guide its relations with neighbours to the south and the east. This new concept does not specify the content of the values that were used during the previous stages of relations. But it has marked a shift to a more inclusive understanding of human rights. That notwithstanding, political rights have still been perceived as the precondition to economic development, while the social and economic rights of ENP citizens have not been recognised as a priority per se (Ghazaryan, 2016: 16-20). Furthermore, as discussed in chapter 4 on ownership and local dynamics, local actors have also perceived the EU's democracy promotion especially in the southern neighbourhood as disregarding local conditions and local values. It is important to note that the "new approach" has not resulted in the establishment of new mechanisms to achieve the ideal type of "deep democracy" (Emerson, 2011). Nevertheless, the differences between the south and the east are noticeable when one compares the eastern association agreements and the Euro-Mediterranean agreements. "Essential elements clauses" constitute the normative framework of the values promoted by the EU in a particular state and they are more onerous in the east "both in terms of the elements considered as essential, as well as in terms of the international standards that form their basis" (Ghazaryan, 2016: 24).

The researchers argue that the given ambiguity of the values that is inherent in the EU's founding Treaties, its legal framework and agreements with the ENP states considerably impedes the Union's ability to promote those values and to pursue a coherent foreign policy towards its neighbours in general (Gstöhl, 2016b; Pech, 2012).

In sum, one should underline that the body of literature analysed in this section tends to focus on the official documents that regulate the EU's policy. Thus, it might present the EU as a single actor. In this respect, the studies do not elaborate on the individual member states' positions regarding EU values during negotiations on the EU Treaties and agreements between the EU and ENP states. This leaves open the question of why the EU has made a choice in favour of such ambiguous definitions of values. One might presume that it was made deliberately to allow the member states to pursue their own foreign policy objectives, which is completely in line with the preservation of the intergovernmental nature of the CFSP. In addition, one should note that the built-in vagueness of the EU values is an important though not a sole reason that impedes the effectiveness of the EU's policies in the neighbourhood. Other factors include the difference in understanding (if not complete rejection) of 'shared' values between ENP partners and the EU, and the challenge posed by other regional actors that promote a different set of values. Yet, what is important is that the ambiguity of values, coupled with the aforementioned factors, encourages selective application of political conditionality in different cases according to the interests of the EU and its member states.

3.2 Security/stability vs. democracy

In this respect, the major policy dilemma that the EU faces is the need to choose the right balance between the promotion of democratic values and the protection of its strategic interests – notably strengthening security and stability in the neighbourhood. When analysing the Wider Europe Communication, ENP Strategy Paper, and 2003 European Security Strategy, one could conclude that the main purpose of the EU was to prevent any 'negative spillover' from the neighbourhood by creating a circle of 'well-governed democratic states'. Thus, the altruistic component of the ENP has been questioned by experts. It also can be argued that the EU's aim to surround itself with economically and politically stable states assumes the creation of a "buffer zone" between the Union and less stable spaces to the south and the east (Zaiotti, 2007; Ghazaryan, 2014; Nielsen and Vilson, 2014). While some authors do not question the status of democracy as one of the main objectives of the EU's external policies (Lavenex and Schimmelfennig, 2011), other scholars consider democracy rather as an element of stability, a necessary factor that enables stability and thus plays an intermediate role within the policy (Stewart, 2011: 607, 610).

The given contradiction is derived from the different perspectives on stability and security: if promoting values in the neighbourhood is a long-term effort, security and stability are short-term needs that the EU often prioritises in its interactions with ENP countries (Hollis, 2012; Dandashly, 2015). Long-term security and stability, however, are not possible without a functioning democracy. As the Lisbon Treaty (Art. 21 TEU) implies a certain flexibility in sequencing different objectives, "democracy promotion has been included within the ENP objectives through the back door" (Ghazaryan, 2014: 29).

In this respect, the ENP was developed to address the concerns of the member states about the possible challenges that their neighbours, both to the east and the south (might) have posed. In the eastern direction, after the 2004 'big bang' enlargement, the EU was facing the risk of political and economic turbulence in the post-Soviet states being transmitted across the shared border (Sadowski, 2013; Wisniewski, 2013). Particularly, the EU was concerned about the potential penetration of criminal networks, corruption, smuggling and trafficking. Also, the EU was worried about the vulnerability of states and hybrid regimes under the influence of Russia. Its attempts to reverse the situation has produced mixed results. The EU has had to take into account concerns of the new member states about Ukraine as an important actor in terms of energy transit, but also as the one that could be used as a buffer zone protecting the newcomers from Russia (Leigh, 2015: 204). A similar approach applies to the MENA region, where the risks of political instability, as well as a threat of terrorism and the trafficking of people, drugs and weapons, are considered to be even greater than in the eastern neighbourhood (Leigh, 2015: 205; Dandashly, 2015: 50).

In a study on why the EU failed to contribute to the democratisation of the southern ENP countries before the Arab Spring, Hollis (2012) argues that the Arab Spring was caused by the EU's policies by default and not by intention. Based on the findings of other researchers and a series of interviews with officials from both the EU and MENA region, Hollis argues that the EU did not act according to its own normative principles and aspirations vis-à-vis the Arab world. Instead, the EU has been consistent in prioritising its security interests over 'shared prosperity' and democracy promotion, and created structured, institutionalised and securitised relations with its southern neighbours, which are not easy to alter and are not conducive to supporting Arab reformers. The Arab governments did not oppose the EU's approach either, mainly for the sake of being given access to the EU market and the opportunity to gain financial and technical assistance (Hollis, 2012; Biscop et al., 2012). Even prior to the Arab Spring protests, the EU concentrated on issues of migration, the rise of fundamentalism and counterterrorism. All the then leaders of the MENA region "shared with the Union an interest in controlling the risk of terrorism locally" (Wouters and Duquet, 2013: 15). In this context, Hollis provides an example of the action plan concluded with Morocco, which envisaged implementation of detailed measures on migration control as one of the conditions for receiving EU financial support (Hollis, 2012: 92-93).

In assessing the role of the EU member states in shaping the EU's policies towards its southern neighbourhood, Witney and Dworkin (2012: 38) note that "for years, the member states instrumentalised the EU to provide cover for the pursuit of disreputable and short-sighted national policies [towards] the countries of North Africa". The aforementioned security-related fields of the ENP were under the control of member states that pursue bilateral policies with ENP states, while the EU institutions were attributed tasks in the sphere of human rights and democracy (Witney and Dworkin, 2012; Biscop et al., 2012; Leigh, 2015; Lehne, 2014). As Leigh notes, it is hard to avoid tensions between the EU and national governments when the EU tries to pursue both objectives: "national ministers become irritated if criticisms by EU officials of a neighbouring country's human rights record jeopardize ongoing bilateral negotiations" (Leigh, 2015: 219). When it comes to conflict resolution, Lehne argues, it is a particular position of one of the member states or its participation in peace talks that has been an obstacle for more active EU engagement (Lehne, 2014). For instance, experts underline the role of the 'big three' in the Mediterranean region: France, Italy and Spain, with a dominant position of the former. In 2010 France provided more financial aid to every North African state than the EU did (Witney and Dworkin, 2012). On the other hand, it is worth mentioning that dependency between the EU and the ENP states might be considered reciprocal. For example, according to Khalifa Isaac (2013: 52), 30.36% of Europe's oil imports come from MENA countries, while over the past decade the southern EU member states' dependence on cheap North African gas (mainly from Libya, Algeria and Egypt) has been increasing.

There is an incompatibility between the common EU interest and the interests of individual member states in various policy frameworks operating in the southern neighbourhood along with the ENP: the Euro-Mediterranean Partnership (launched in 1995), the Union for the Mediterranean (2008), and the Partnership for Democracy and Shared Prosperity with the Southern Mediterranean (2011, part of the ENP) (Leigh, 2015: 210-211). As Schumacher (2011) argues, simultaneous use of the principles of regionalism, bilateralism, project-based cooperation and inter-regionalism only adds to the present fragmented nature of the EU's policies. According to him, "the fact that approaches, initiatives, partnerships, policies and so on are replaced over and over again merely reflects the short-sightedness and disagreement that still exist among EU governments with regard to the role the EU should play in its 'near abroad' – in spite of all the treaties that were supposed to elevate its actorness to a higher level" (Schumacher, 2011: 114).

The Arab Spring disrupted the consensus between the EU and its ENP countries in the south, and has shown that a 'security and stability first' approach has not prevented the region from falling prey to political turmoil. The initial reaction of the EU institutions and member states provided additional evidence of the incoherence of EU policies caused by divergent interests of the Union and its members (Schumacher, 2011; Witney and Dworkin, 2012). The EU adopted different approaches in different cases (Biscop, 2016), and in the most of them it chose 'wait-and-see' tactics and was reluctant to call political leaders to step down even after they used violence against the protesters (Raik, 2012).

The EU's fragmented nature and its reluctance to support political changes in the neighbourhood were particularly evident during the uprising in Tunisia in January 2011. While the majority of European leaders decided not to hurry with a public assessment of the situation in the country, France (by way of its minister for foreign affairs) offered technical support and expertise on managing the protests to the regime of Zine el-Abidine Ben Ali. During the active phase of the protests, the EU advocated the need for dialogue, and only after Ben Ali was ousted from his office did the EU give a statement on its support for the aspirations of the Tunisian people (Schumacher, 2011; Raik, 2012).

The events in Egypt followed a similar pattern. The country is considered an important regional actor due to the size of its population, its geographical location and, in particular, its role in containing conflict between Israel and Hamas in Gaza (Leigh, 2015). Also, the EU regarded its leader, Hosni Mubarak, as a regional strongman committed to the fight against Islamic extremism, and therefore advocated a democratic transition with Mubarak staying in the presidential office contrary to the desire of Egyptians. Despite the increased violence against the opposition, EU leaders were hesitant (in contrast to US President Barack Obama) to demand Mubarak's resignation (Schumacher, 2011; Raik, 2012; Khalifa Isaac, 2013). Yet in the case of Libya, European leaders decided to support the opposition to Gaddafi's regime with military intervention

(Biscop, 2016). Nevertheless, the process did not go smoothly: while having agreed on the need for Gaddafi's resignation, EU leaders were hesitant to follow French President Nicolas Sarkozy's example and recognise the Libyan National Transition Council. The disagreement about the introduction of a non-fly zone and the subsequent decision of Germany to withhold itself from participating in the NATO-led military operation once more exposed divisions within the EU (Zajac, 2015). The same reason explains the EU's failure to articulate a consolidated position and react in a more determined manner to the violent suppression of the protests in Syria in March 2011 (Schumacher, 2011; Khalifa Isaac, 2013).

In this regard, according to Raik (2012), the EU's internal debates did not lead to significant reconceptualisation of the EU's approach to democracy promotion and a switch to more proactive strategies. The Brussels institutions "adroitly filled the policy vacuum" that emerged within the EU in light of the Arab uprisings (Witney and Dworkin, 2012: 40). Soon after the revolutions in Tunisia, Egypt and Libya the EU prioritised security, stability, migration, fighting the rise of fundamentalism and counter-terrorism rather than shift its attention to supporting the advancement of the democratisation process, supposedly also owing to the increase of political instability and growing socio-economic concerns in the southern Mediterranean countries (Dandashly, 2015). For instance, the post-Arab Spring mobility partnerships sought to combat "irregular migration and implement effective readmission and return policy" (Dias, 2014: 54).

In sum, the literature is straightforward in its conclusions about the EU's priorities: when facing the crisis (or a chance of its emergence) in the neighbourhood, the EU and the member states focus their efforts on preventing any possible negative spillovers, often at the expense of promoting the EU's values. Furthermore, the member states tend to prioritise geostrategic interests in relations with the ENP partners, which in turn considerably undermines the EU's normative agenda (for more on vertical coherence, please see section 7.3).

3.3 (Functional) cooperation with non-democratic regimes

It is often emphasised that, in order to maintain political stability in the neighbourhood, the EU has opted for engagement with authoritarian leaders rather than choosing a side in the domestic conflict and openly supporting challengers of autocrats' rule. For example, the EU assumed the role of mediator in Egypt between the military and former President Mohammed Morsi of the Muslim Brotherhood (Morillas, 2015) and even "quietly aligned" with President Abdel Fattah el-Sisi (Biscop, 2016: 8). Another case widely mentioned in the literature is the introduction of the joint presidency (with European and Arab heads of states) as an institutional solution to save the Union for the Mediterranean from further regress when compared with the Euro-Mediterranean Partnership. The first presidency was co-chaired by French President Sarkozy and President Mubarak of Egypt, although the former was also criticised for his famous handshake with Syria's President Assad during the launch of the Union for the Mediterranean (Hollis, 2012; Biscop et al., 2012). When it comes to the eastern dimension of the neighbourhood, the case of cooperation with Ilham Aliyev's regime is often analysed (Kobzova and Alieva, 2012; Hale, 2012). Azerbaijan is considered a crucial actor for the EU as it can contribute to the diversification of its energy sources, while it is also not in the interest of the Union to have another regional military conflict, between Azerbaijan and Armenia over Nagorno-Karabakh (Ghazaryan, 2014; Merabishvili, 2015).

One could find other examples of the EU choosing pragmatic interests over values, for example, in trade with non-EU states in specific sectors. In her recent study of arms exports by EU member states to 20 autocratic regimes in the immediate neighbourhood and beyond in the period from 2003 to 2013, Bosse's (2016: 297-298) findings are as follows:

1) the majority of the EU's criteria on arms exports and conditions that have to be met to grant export licenses to a particular country is formally guided by moral norms and principles (compliance with international law and human rights by an importer);

2) the majority of arms embargoes has been justified by referencing to those benchmarks (with the exception of Belarus, where there is a wider appeal to such standards of the EU as respect of democracy and rule of law);

3) those moral benchmarks do not significantly influence the EU member states' decisions on exporting arms to third countries – the main decisive factor is a level of demand; and

4) the EU and its member states are eager to stop arms exports to an authoritarian regime only if there is a sudden, and visible, negative change in the human rights situation, such as extreme violence against opposition and mass murders.

In this regard, the demonstration of different attitudes towards undemocratic regimes, when choosing or balancing between democratisation and stabilisation policy options, undermines the EU's normative agenda (Biscop, 2016). As a result, the EU's normative power image has not only been questioned abroad but also challenged by domestic publics within the Union. For instance, European public opinion was very critical about EU governments' initial reactions to the revolutions in Tunisia and Egypt. The public uproar in France even led to the resignation of the aforementioned French foreign minister after her statements in support of former President Ben Ali (Biscop et al., 2012). As Witney and Dworkin note, European policy in the Mediterranean for years was guided by a peculiar Faustian pact – "quiet European complicity with the autocracies, in exchange for their cooperation in keeping their teeming populations and disturbing religion at arm's length" (Witney and Dworkin, 2012: 6). Under pressure to democratise, many leaders have found a way to "upgrade authoritarianism" by introducing or imitating a limited range of reforms in certain sectors while keeping the political sphere as an exclusive domain for their own rule. As a consequence, according to Schumacher, "the ENP's underlying objective, i.e. to break the pattern of 'stubborn authoritarianism' and contribute gradually to a transition towards representative and liberal democracies, was systematically bypassed" (Schumacher, 2011: 110). Moreover, the situation, in which cooperation and conditionality are driven more by EU rational interests than any request for good governance and democracy, has not changed since the Arab Spring (Biscop, 2016: 8).

There is nonetheless a body of literature that does not share this point of view regarding reasons and modes of cooperation between the EU and non-democratic governments. For instance, acknowledging that democracy promotion and maintaining stability/security are two conflicting goals when dealing with authoritarian regimes, Freyburg proposes to utilise so-called functional cooperation, which can serve both goals simultaneously (Freyburg, 2012; Freyburg et al., 2015). Taking as an example EU–Morocco cooperation on water issues, the researcher argues that functional cooperation on the micro- or meso-levels of administrative governance can bring, first of all, social and economic well-being to the population of a partner country, thus helping the regime to maintain political stability by preventing the possibility of social unrest against it. Second, functional cooperation will spread democratic norms and practices and increase citizens' participation on the ground. Therefore, functional cooperation is regarded as a compromise: it does not challenge the political power of an authoritarian leader while assisting the leader in a fight against social and economic grievances, and at the same time, it creates so-called democratic enclaves within governmental administration (Freyburg, 2012; Freyburg et al., 2015).

Biscop (2016) advocates the same idea, arguing that any non-democratic regime will be interested in such cooperation to improve equality among its citizens because it will increase domestic stability. Nevertheless, according to the researcher, while not trying to impose democracy and change the regime, the EU has to establish concrete red lines for cooperation with any non-democratic regime in terms of compliance of the latter with principles of human rights.

In the same vein, recognising that the EU does not use its main instrument – membership conditionality – mostly because of 'enlargement fatigue', Lavenex and Schimmelfennig (2011) propose a governance approach towards ENP states. They call for a given model to complement the two traditional approaches (linkage and leverage) by operating within particular policy fields and increasing the cooperation among the public administration structures of the EU and the target state in specific sectors. Furthermore, the model operates by 'democratic governance', which focuses more on democratic standards (transparency, accountability and participation) within public policy and administration rather than elections and parliaments. At the same time, the model is embedded in the EU's 'external governance' when the EU's partner state adapts its legal framework and internal policies to the EU *acquis* (Lavenex and Schimmelfennig, 2011; 2013). Thus, some scholars argue that the EU should increase its support for domestic reform by developing more training courses for the judiciary, policing and security personnel, incentivising reform of electoral laws and supporting cooperation between the public and private sectors (Al-Anani et al., 2011).

Despite the fact that Lavenex and Schimmelfennig (2011) acknowledge the necessity of elaborating an alternative approach that corresponds to the existing ENP, it is not clear why the ruling elites remain hesitant to pursue democratic reforms at the level of legislature and elections, as these reforms would increase transparency and accountability within particular governmental agencies and ministries. Wetzel and Orbie (2012) found that in the EU's support of state capacity building, administrative effectiveness is not always compatible with the aims of democratisation. It can even lead to the strengthening of autocratic leadership by improving the functions of its bureaucratic apparatus (courts, for example) without providing their independence. But such an approach is in line with the 'default substance' of EU democracy promotion: it is output-oriented, in other words, it focuses on the strengthening of government and its administration rather than on development of the public sphere and empowering non-state actors (input-oriented). It also primarily concentrates on the socio-economic development of its partners while paying considerably less attention to such partial regimes of democracy as 'horizontal accountability' (the system of checks and balances) and 'effective power to govern' (the absence of tutelary powers and reserved domains) (Wetzel and Orbie, 2015: 236). As Biscop notes, "the European belief in its idealist agenda is sincere, but its pragmatic application is a reality too. It is also mostly un-avowed. The result is a lack of coherence and consistency" (Biscop, 2016: 9).

In a nutshell, researchers argue that because of its strategic objectives in the fields of security, energy and economy, the EU does not shun cooperation with autocrats ruling in its neighbourhood. This in turn undermines the EU's normative identity, both domestically and externally. That notwithstanding, there is a body of literature that argues in favour of engagement with non-democratic regimes in spheres that directly do not a pose a threat to the political power of their leaders but do facilitate diffusion of the EU's norms and practices to local and meso-levels of governmental structures. In contrast, another school of thought argues that such cooperation does not lead to the creation of 'democratic enclaves' within authoritarian political systems but strengthens the latter. In this respect, it should be noted that further empirical and case-study research should be done to evaluate the validity of arguments advocated by representatives of 'governance'/'functional cooperation' models, and if these modes could lead to incremental democratic changes within ENP societies without provoking their non-democratic leaders.

3.4 Conclusion

In general, researchers underline that the EU's policies towards its neighbourhood are characterised by the inherent conflict between values and interests. The majority of studies argue that the EU tends to prioritise the latter over the former, especially when dealing with non-democratic regimes. In addition, while the EU operates with notions of 'shared' and 'common' values, one could argue that these are poorly defined and ambiguous. For example, one of the cornerstone values of the EU, democracy, which is both a principle and an objective of EU relations with neighbouring states, has an all-embracing character that might not be in line with some member state models of democracy. The ambiguity of values is reinforced by other factors, such as their conflict with the local values dominating in some ENP societies and competition from the side of other regional players that, deliberately or involuntarily, counterbalance the EU's influence.

In this respect, researchers are sceptical regarding the EU's ability to effectively combine the pursuit of both objectives of the ENP – democracy and stability – for a number of reasons. First, because promotion of democracy might bring destabilisation to non-democratic countries and increase the level of uncertainty connected to regime change, the EU prefers to downgrade its normative agenda in relations with autocracies. Thus, the EU is not willing to risk losing stability, even in the short term, for the sake of the more distant goal of an ideal equilibrium, in which democracy and stability coincide (Grimm and Leininger, 2012; Dandashly, 2015). Moreover, the EU's reluctance to promote political change grows when non-democratic regimes already show some signs of domestic instability. In such cases, the EU is keen to focus on the "stabilisation" agenda in its policies towards a particular regime (Börzel and van Hüllen, 2014). Second, a high level of stability is not a necessary precondition to pursue democracy promotion aims. There should be a minimum level of liberalisation in a partner state where the EU should have its own allies (liberal political elites, opposition and civil society) to support necessary reforms. For example, relatively high levels of political liberalisation in Moldova and Ukraine do allow the EU to have a more balanced agenda in terms of democracy and stability compared with other ENP states, especially those situated in the south. Therefore, the "democracy-stability" dilemma might be solved when a partner state is already going through the process of political transition to a more democratic regime and the two objectives reinforce each other (Börzel and van Hüllen, 2014: 1044).

Yet, several observations should be made regarding the existing consensus among scholars on the domination of strategic pragmatism over the normative agenda within the EU's external policies. Indeed, the literature takes a clear stance on this issue and is critical towards the EU's priorities within the ENP. In some cases, researchers themselves make normative claims while assessing the EU's approach towards the neighbourhood. It should be noted that in general scholars tend to draw conclusions about the ineffectiveness of the ENP and its discrepancies with its stated goals based on the negative results of political transformations that have taken place in the partner countries. In other words, the ENP is recognised as an ineffective tool because it has failed to achieve its major goal – creating stable, prosperous and well-governed states near its borders – particularly owing to the abandonment of its normative agenda. However, the major thrust of experts' criticism is not directed at the EU for having legitimate pragmatic interests in its neighbourhood, but at its unwillingness to openly acknowledge those interests while preserving its normative rhetoric in relations with its partners. One could argue that the EU's actions in the neighbourhood are not expected to be driven solely by a normative agenda, but a proper balance should be found between values and interests (which in turn should be clearly defined and agreed among all EU actors).

In this regard, more attention should be paid to the individual understanding by member states of what the EU's values and interests are. More specifically, it should be noted that researchers mainly look at individual member states' strategic interests in the neighbourhood rather than analyse their activities to promote the EU's values and various types of assistance provided to ENP societies. It should also be acknowledged that the EU should not be considered an actor that holds complete responsibility for every failure of ENP states to become full-fledged democracies. It is already recognised by researchers that there is a more sophisticated interplay between various endogenous and exogenous forces that influence the attitudes and regime trajectories of ENP societies.

4. Ownership and Local Dynamics

The lack of tailoring EU policies to local and domestic conditions is often seen as one of the primary deficiencies of the ENP. This chapter elaborates on two particularly prominent issues with regard to local dynamics: the lack of differentiation in ENP policies and the lack of local ownership.

The bulk of the literature discusses the principle of differentiation, addressing the specific tailoring of EU neighbourhood policies to the needs of each of the partners (Inayeh and Forbrig, 2015; Mocanu, 2013; Delcour, 2015a, 2015b; Tocci, 2014; Sololenko and Hallgren, 2015). Generally, a more tailor-made approach has been proposed to increase the effectiveness of the ENP and its adaptation to local conditions, based on individual assessments of each country's progress (Langbein and Börzel, 2013; Harpaz, 2014; Mocanu, 2013). To this end, Delcour (2015a) recommends strengthening the EU's bilateral track of the ENP while maintaining its multilateral platforms of cooperation with the ENP partners. Maurer and Simao (2013) furthermore discuss the issue of reconciling the promotion of common values and sufficient differentiation.

The lack of 'ownership' and the broader dialogue between the EU as a democracy promoter and the partner society is also identified as a basic deficiency in the EU's democracy promotion towards the ENP countries (Jonasson, 2013). In addition, the relation between the EU's democracy promotion and the domestic political situation in the ENP countries is analysed by a substantive part of the literature (Sasse, 2013; Orbie and Wetzel, 2015; Maggi, 2016; Giusti, 2016). Sasse (2013) argues that the consideration of domestic political conditions is fundamental when assessing external promotion of democratic reforms, also given the wide range of international linkages. As has been discussed with regard to sectoral convergence, the effectiveness of policy convergence often depends on the interaction and relationship between foreign actors and domestic elites; nevertheless, the literature often does not pay enough attention to the priorities and preferences of domestic actors (Samokhvalov, 2015; Ademmer, 2015). Particularly in the case of tensions between the EU and Russia in the eastern neighbourhood, domestic politics and power dynamics are in many cases underestimated or omitted by the literature in consideration of the influence of external actors on domestic policies (Dimitrova and Dragneva, 2013).

Several recent studies assess how the EU's policies and instruments are perceived by its partners on the ground, thus emphasising the necessity of the continuing dialogue between the EU and domestic stakeholders on improving/adjusting the EU's approach (ECFR, 2015; Solodkyy and Sharlay, 2015). Beyond the cooperation with national governments, the literature also reiterates the importance of non-governmental initiatives and partnerships with civil society and local stakeholders (Solodkyy and Sharlay, 2015; Kaca et al., 2014; Dennison et al., 2011).

4.1 Tailoring to local needs?

Differentiation is discussed by a number of sources not only in terms of distinguishing between southern and eastern neighbourhoods, but also increasingly in terms of tailoring the EU's policies and instruments to the individual needs of ENP countries. Especially with regard to the southern neighbourhood, the literature points to the problem of implementing a one-size-fits-all approach and insufficient differentiation between the policies implemented in each of the partner countries corresponding to local conditions (Henökl and Stemberger, 2016; Mocanu, 2013). In both the southern and the eastern neighbourhoods, however, insufficient differentiation has constituted a recurring aspect in the ENP literature.

In the southern neighbourhood, calls for more tailor-made approaches within the ENP were primarily made in response to the Arab Spring, which for many authors demonstrated the need to reassess the basis of the EU's engagement with Arab countries and the southern Mediterranean (Dandashly, 2015; Tocci, 2014; Comelli,

2013). According to Dandashly (2015), the assessment of local circumstances, including economic and political conditions, is particularly influential with regard to EU democracy support in the MENA region and the EU's approach to political reform. In the case of Arab countries and even more specifically in relation to the rise of political Islam and Islamist parties, the EU's approach in reflecting local conditions and the dynamics between local actors has been described as problematic (Tocci, 2014; Seeberg, 2014; Wouters et al., 2013; Grant, 2011). While it can be said that the MENA region is one of the most heterogeneous ones in terms of local conditions and political characterisations, the diversification reflecting these conditions is largely missing from the EU's approach to the region and its development under the ENP (Pace, 2014).

The need to reassess the EU's policies towards the southern neighbourhood stems from changes in the political conditions caused by the Arab Spring, which produced a "more differentiated, complex and unstable Middle Eastern reality" (Seeberg, 2014: 453). Although it can be suggested that the region had previously been just as diverse in its political, economic and other characterisations, the Arab Spring produced new conditions and drew the EU's attention to the role of civil society as a driving force behind political change (Pace, 2014). In light of the new political systems and conditions among civil society, the EU should pay more attention to domestic politics and develop new partnerships with domestic and local authorities (Fernández and Behr, 2013). According to Tocci (2014: 5), the Arab Spring flagged a time for the EU to develop new objectives of the ENP while "tailoring the EU's policy instruments (...) to realistic objectives that reflect existing realities".

In general terms, two reasons are given for the EU's inability to differentiate its policies in the neighbourhood according to the general needs of partner countries and local conditions on the ground. First, this could be caused by a conscious preference for a more broadly defined (universal) policy approach, or second, by the inability to grasp the variations in local conditions and national needs, and the failure to translate them into effective policy. Similarly, Wouters et al. (2013) argue that in some instances official communication from EU bodies does not reflect conditions on the ground in the ENP countries, reflecting either a decision by the EU to focus on its own priority areas or a flawed understanding of local conditions. The flawed official communication, however, does not necessarily reflect the actual analysis of the EU institutions and the member states.

While in his 'review of the review' of the ENP in 2011 Emerson (2011: 4) demonstrates "glaring contradictions and lack of a sound analytical basis" for the DCFTA and a missing understanding of local conditions, several authors argue that the EU instead chooses to prioritise its own interests over the local needs of ENP stakeholders (Hollis, 2012; Dandashly, 2015; Grant, 2011).

Beyond basing differentiation specifically on domestic conditions, Fernández and Behr (2013) argues that the EU needs to develop new policies and strategies to reflect specific challenges that derive from regional and trans-regional geopolitical dynamics, such as the revival of sectarian politics, worsening Sunni–Shia relations and security spillovers caused by the conflict in Syria and Iraq. Seeberg (2014) confirms that several of the domestic challenges that occur specifically in the southern neighbourhood, such as polarisation between Islamist and secular parties and their constituencies, can be attributed to regional and trans-regional dynamics. Reflecting these concerns with respect to a wider Middle East that appears to be in free fall, Blockmans (2016b) calls for a more conflict-sensitive approach by the EU,

> to support those in the region who are trying to find peaceful, constructive solutions, and to stick with them. The challenge is to secure the lands they inhabit; establish effective development policies in close partnership with them; address underlying issues of governing, corruption and repression; and find ways to help restructure their economies, in a functional way, opening up to other stable parts of the region.

In the case of the eastern neighbourhood, this relates primarily to the changing dynamics between the EU, the ENP countries (particularly their political and business elites) and Russia, which is discussed in chapter 6 on external (f)actors.

To conclude, there is an overwhelming consensus that the ENP needs to move towards further differentiation to address country-specific needs. Yet, there are differences as to how this should be achieved and to what extent the policies should be differentiated. Furthermore, several sources share the concern that the EU seems to design its policies based on its own experiences and benchmarks, without taking into account realities on the ground. The 2015 Review of the ENP put a significant emphasis on stronger and more differentiated partnerships.

4.2   Eastern neighbourhood

According to Delcour and Wolczuk (2013b), implementation of some provisions of the association agreements with the eastern ENP partner countries has often had an impact on domestic power structures and the dynamics between local interest groups and actors, especially in politically sensitive areas. Focusing on the case of Armenia, they further argue that "implementing these rules would infringe on the vested interests of powerful business players, who control domestic markets in a monopolistic way and have a strong and influential presence in the governments or parliaments of the partner countries" (Delcour and Wolczuk, 2013b: 3-4). A comprehensive assessment of the domestic dynamics and situation of the partner countries in the eastern neighbourhood is therefore considered just as imperative as in the case of the southern ENP dimension.

As previously stated, the concern over disregard of local conditions and dynamics by the EU has been demonstratively present among local stakeholders, in both the countries of the Eastern Partnership and the southern neighbourhood (Dostál et al., 2015; Dennison et al., 2011). Based on a survey conducted among numerous experts within the EaP, Dostál et al. (2015: 11) argue that "despite encompassing a number of highly distinct countries, the Eastern Partnership initiative lacks a sensible forked approach responding to their inner history, politics and socio-economic conditions". A similar argument is presented in further studies, which point out that the EU has paid insufficient attention to local dynamics as well as the individual needs and motivations of its partners (Najšlová et al., 2013).

Tocci (2014: 6) argues that in the eastern neighbourhood the EU primarily needs to differentiate between the "frontrunners" of the EaP that have concluded the association agreements with the European Union, namely Ukraine, Moldova and Georgia, and the remaining three countries, Armenia, Azerbaijan and Belarus. While each of these countries has achieved a different level of integration with the EU, the prevailing emphasis should be placed on state-building and strengthening the domestic political institutions. Securing the "basic elements of functioning statehood" should be considered a first step towards deeper and more effective integration with the countries of the EaP.

Moreover, the conditionality should be tailored by the EU to the capabilities of the domestic authorities of individual countries. According to Kaca et al. (2014), these conditions are often not shaped properly, are too broad or too ambitious, and are based to some extent on the insufficient capacity of national administrations and a lack of established dialogue with local stakeholders. Based on their research on EU budget support initiatives in EaP countries, the authors identify the lack of consultation with local stakeholders besides national governments as one of the biggest constraints in the programming periods of such initiatives, which consequently hinders effective implementation of reforms (Kaca et al., 2014). Therefore, the authors recommend the introduction of comprehensive consultations with various stakeholders, including civil society organisations, political elites and other interest groups on initiatives that target broader social reform.

Scholarship focusing on the eastern neighbourhood and the application of joint ownership and differentiation in the eastern ENP dimension highlights the necessity of paying attention to the impact of ENP initiatives on domestic power structures and the needs and capabilities of local actors. Both the southern and eastern neighbourhoods have seen an increasing contrast among the individual countries, their needs, interests and capabilities, and the literature overwhelmingly agrees on the need to strengthen the concept of differentiation within the ENP framework. Data gathered among stakeholders in the eastern neighbourhood also shows that those stakeholders wish to see more tailoring to local conditions and taking account of local interests in the development of future instruments and joint initiatives (Dostál et al., 2015).

Furthermore, Kaca et al. (2014) highlight the impact that the lack of comprehensive consultations between the EU and local stakeholders other than national government representatives can have on both the programming and implementation stages of EU initiatives in the EaP countries. While the EaP is becoming more diversified in terms of local needs and experiences, the lack of dialogue between the EU and local stakeholders threatens to obstruct the effectiveness of the financial and budgetary support instruments as well as other initiatives that are directed at social reform more broadly.

4.3 Joint ownership

Several studies analyse the role of the concept of local ownership and 'joint ownership'. (Delcour, 2015a; Korosteleva, 2011, 2012; Maurer & Simao, 2013; Shapovalova and Youngs, 2012). During the latest ENP Review, the concept of joint or mutual ownership was highlighted as one of the main pillars of the ENP, demonstrating the strengthening of mutual relationships between the EU and its partners and the intention to move away from traditional top-down policies under the ENP. The concept of mutual ownership has been designed to move away from the traditional, hierarchical relationship structures between the EU and the ENP countries towards a strengthened partnership (Korosteleva, 2013).

The literature is widely supportive of the emphasis on mutual ownership, i.e. Delcour (2015a: 6) notes that "there cannot be any sustainable reforms without strong local ownership (and therefore adjustment to local circumstances)". According to Korosteleva (2013: 11), the new approach of joint ownership and focus on a comprehensive partnership nevertheless requires two important steps without which the approach falls short of effective change, and these are "institutionalisation of the new governance structure" and "learning about 'the other', to mobilise partners' support for reciprocal and sustainable cooperation".

Despite the importance attached to the concept, the substance of the term 'partnership' itself has remained ambiguous and ill-defined, which might, according to some studies, have a profound impact on the credibility and effectiveness of the EU as a normative actor (Korosteleva, 2011, 2012; Schimmelfennig, 2012). Lavenex and Schimmelfennig (2011: 902) state that these concerns have been to a large extent justified, as the development as well as credibility and effectiveness of the EU's policies is hampered by the lack of "clear conceptual underpinnings" and "well-defined democratic conditions". Furthermore, Korosteleva (2011: 244) argues that "there appears to be marked continuity under the Eastern Partnership in both the format of engagement and the prioritisation of EU ownership of rhetoric and actions". According to Maurer and Simao (2013: 12), joint ownership between the EU and its ENP partners can further be affected by "the reluctance of member states to discuss issues more profoundly, such as aspects of trade liberalization and migration facilitation".

Najšlová et al. (2013: 3) note that especially in the eastern neighbourhood, the overarching policy frameworks – including the ENP, and the EaP and instruments and initiatives that are attached to them – are in many cases "incomprehensible" to local stakeholders, "let alone citizens". Joint ownership is thus often precluded by strategies designed in a way that alienates local stakeholders and civil society representatives from engaging with the ENP.

Delcour (2015a) states that the EU has predominantly modelled the ENP according to its own experience, exporting its own model of economic integration and regional cooperation, and has evaluated the ENP according to the input rather than the output of its policies. Consequently, Delcour (2015a: 5) argues for a "shift of paradigm", meaning that the EU should "tailor its policies to partner countries' needs and circumstances". Local conditions also play a role in legitimising democracy promotion and the kind of negative conditionality that is used against some regimes in both the south and the east against human rights abuses and lack of progress in democratisation. According to Dennison and Dworkin (2011: 3), the EU should "engage in a battle of ideas – in other words make a case for human rights and democracy that is rooted in local concerns rather than Western political models".

The perception that the EU would support democracy for the sake of its own interests is also reiterated especially in the case of Tunisia. Dennison et al. (2011: 2) quote Tunisians describing their experience of the EU's support for former President Ben Ali: "the EU wanted democracy for itself but not for us". Pace (2014: 975) goes as far as to suggest that "because the EU was not questioning its vision on the MENA and thereby not dealing directly with the social, political and economic needs of the people, it was distrusted and mocked for its supposed support for democracy in the region".

The perception that the ENP does not sufficiently reflect the experiences and needs of the local population has been frequently highlighted with respect to the southern dimension of the ENP. While Neuvonen (2015) suggests that prior to the Arab Spring the ENP was mainly perceived as an instrument for strengthening economic cooperation between the EU and the ENP countries, the aftermath of the revolts and recurring conflicts in the region has brought migration management to the very core of the EU's foreign and neighbourhood policy agenda. This has inevitably been reflected in and has perhaps even characterised the EU's relations with the southern ENP countries ever since. Tailoring the strategies and instruments used within the framework of the ENP to local conditions and needs is nevertheless considered to be just as pivotal to the long-term stabilisation of the EU's neighbourhood (Tocci, 2014).

Overall the literature is very supportive of the increased emphasis on mutual or joint ownership. As the following section shows, top-down dynamics in partnerships with ENP countries can significantly hinder the implementation of fundamental reforms, especially with respect to democracy promotion. The literature is not definite on whether the lack of joint ownership is more relevant to the eastern or southern neighbourhoods. However, the challenge the EU faces in understanding local conditions is emphasised more in relation to the southern neighbourhood. In particular, many authors claim that the EU did not effectively react to the uprisings in the Arab world, thus undermining its partnership with the southern neighbourhood countries in the following years. The literature shows that the formulation of joint policy frameworks matters greatly and more cooperation with local stakeholders is desired. This is actually very important as the research shows that the benchmarks set by the EU are often incomprehensible and do not address local needs and interests.

4.4 Local ownership and civil society support

Ownership plays a significant role in the EU's relationship with civil society in the respective ENP countries and several authors examine the role of civil society in ENP initiatives (Boiten, 2015; Junemann, 2012; Kostanyan, 2014b; Shapovalova, 2015; Shapovalova and

Youngs, 2012). Although the EU has attached considerable importance to civil society in its recent policy and strategy papers, Boiten (2015) argues that at the conceptual level the EU's understanding of and approach towards civil society organisations significantly limits their capacity and potential to contribute to the democratisation process by framing their role exclusively in political terms. The underlying conceptualisations of such foundational terms as 'civil society' and 'democratisation' itself can form the basis of flawed assumptions and strategies that do not take into account local experiences and perceptions. Opposing the idea that civil society has been placed at the core of the EU's policy documents, Pace (2014) argues that in reality the EU's understanding of political reform and democratisation has been one driven by economic liberalisation and reform.

According to Junemann (2012), prior to the Arab Spring, civil society especially in the MENA region was perceived as lacking the necessary development and experience to make a case for itself against the autocratic regimes existing in many countries at that time. After the Arab Spring, the EU needed to reconceptualise its approach to civil society in general and to the growing number of civil society organisations across the region in particular. Despite the seeming interest in civil society promotion and its central role in many of the EU's strategy documents, in reality areas such as market liberalisation and security have been given priority over support for civil society (Boiten, 2015).

The literature suggests that local ownership plays a significant role in democracy promotion in the European neighbourhood and thus the EU has previously attempted to introduce reforms to the EaP to contribute to a more "bottom-up and locally-driven" democratisation process (Shapovalova and Youngs, 2012: 1). A significant shift in the EU's democracy-promotion strategy in the European neighbourhood was introduced in 2007 with the Non-State Actors and Local Authorities Development initiative under the Development Cooperation Instrument (Shapovalova and Youngs, 2012). In the southern neighbourhood, a turn towards civil society as a driving force behind democratisation was reintroduced at the centre of the EU's strategies in the region after the events of the Arab Spring (Boiten, 2015). Although democracy promotion has significantly increased the attention given to civil society actors and organisations, changes in the relevant instruments have ultimately not achieved greater effectiveness in democracy promotion within the framework of the ENP (Shapovalova and Youngs, 2012).

The literature dealing with the role of civil society organisations and democracy support clearly demonstrates the lack of emphasis on joint ownership and how it hinders the contribution that civil society can make to the democratisation process in the ENP countries. While democratisation constitutes one of the focal points of the ENP, based on the values and principles it represents, its approach to civil society organisations has been fundamentally flawed. Surprisingly, there is not a large number of sources that empirically examine the EU's approach to civil society development within the framework of the ENP.

4.5 Eurocentrism: A clash with local/regional values

Consideration of local dynamics and ownership inevitably involves the question of how the EU sees and incorporates local and regional values into its instruments and policy frameworks. While interests play a significant role in the EU's relations with the ENP states, one of the most underestimated problems in the promotion of the EU's 'milieu' goals is confidence in the universality of the EU values. As Leigh notes, "the inspiration for the ENP was pragmatic, (...) but it also claimed to be based on 'shared values'. In fact, shared values were an aspiration rather than a reality in most partner countries. The gap between aspiration and reality proved to be one of the ENP's main deficiencies" (Leigh, 2015: 206-207).

In this respect, researchers critically assess the notion of 'shared values' that is commonly used in official EU documents. The ENP Strategy Paper includes general references to such values as "respect for human dignity, liberty, democracy, equality, the rule of law and respect for human rights" (European Commission, 2004: 12). Thus, the ENP highlights the universal nature of these values as they correspond with many of those respected by international organisations (Korosteleva, 2012; Kochenov and Basheska, 2015). Nevertheless, according to Korosteleva, there are several tensions between the logic of partnership and the values promoted by the ENP. First, in addition to confusion and interchangeable use in the documents of two different meanings of 'shared' (having ownership) and 'common' (typical), a question about substance (which values?) arises. A list of values in the EU documents is not exhaustive, while definitions of values are vague and allows different interpretations by different actors (Korosteleva, 2012: 30).

Second, there is a concern regarding ownership of the values (whose?). As Korosteleva argues, while the understanding of the EU as a "community of values" is contested owing to different visions of values among member states, the EU has not achieved much success in legitimising these values as universal ones at the international level (Korosteleva, 2012). Moreover, the EU claims that the EU concept of 'common values' is a universal one (Korosteleva, 2012; Gstöhl, 2016b). Thus, it provides the EU with additional arguments to promote its values abroad while appealing to their universal character. It is argued that the eastern neighbourhood countries do accept (at least, partially) these values as universal, however, it is highly questionable whether the states of the MENA region do so. Electoral democracy in those countries, as Leigh notes, might come together with a set of different values (particularly inspired by religion) that might be in contradiction with the values prevailing in the EU (e.g. the rights of women, children and minorities, freedom of expression) (Leigh, 2015). In this regard, as Soler i Lecha and Tarragona (2015: 3) note, a legitimate desire of the EU to promote its model of liberal democracy "inevitably collides with an Arab world where, as elsewhere, not all democrats are liberal and not all liberals are democrats". In addition, these partners do not even expect to be invited to join the EU, unlike their eastern colleagues. Thus, their willingness and readiness to accept EU 'shared values' are questionable (Witney and Dworkin, 2012; Leigh, 2015). What is more, according to Leonard, the Arab uprisings are partly "about people claiming democratic rights to emancipate themselves from the traditional influence of the West, rather than trying to join it" (Leonard, 2014).

One of the most critical issues is that the 'shared values' are used as a conditionality element in relations with ENP states; as a basis for any cooperation and assumed to be already shared by partners, values are still promoted to those partners by the EU

(Korosteleva, 2012; Gstöhl, 2016b). Moreover, Art. 21(1) TEU brought even more confusion as it requires the Union to seek to build partnerships with third countries "which share the principles on which it is founded" (Gstöhl, 2016b). Thus, the neighbouring countries are associated with the "shared values" (Gstöhl, 2016b). Art. 8(1) TEU requires partners to adopt specifically EU values in order to have the opportunity for cooperation (Korosteleva, 2012: 32). In general, the use of shared values as a precondition for cooperation by the EU does not comply with a principal of partnership, whereby two actors develop together a set of values and rules (Korosteleva, 2013).

Finally, the European Union does not take into account the fact that

> the current international environment offers little room for [the] EU to exercise some decisive normative leadership as the EU is not unique when it comes to promoting a substantive and holistic conception of the rule of law or financing actions that seek to increase compliance with particular sub-components of the rule of law such as access to justice and an independent judiciary (Pech, 2012: 48).

While Pech addresses the issue of other Western actors that pursue similar goals to those of the EU (OSCE and the Council of Europe), there are regional forces that would like to undermine or promote a different set of values (or are simply an example to follow) in the European neighbourhood, and the EU should not ignore such actors. For instance, following the Arab Spring, the Turkish model of political and economic development gained massive popularity among citizens of countries in the MENA region (Soler i Lecha and Tarragona, 2015). In addition, there is a growing number of those who have positive images of Saudi Arabia and consider its model of government suitable for their own country. The list of those powers that are found attractive or try to export their own set of values also includes China, Qatar and Iran. For example, Mohamed Morsi, after being elected to the office of Egyptian president, made his first official visits to Saudi Arabia, China and Iran before travelling to any European country (Soler i Lecha and Tarragona, 2015). In the eastern neighbourhood the major contender for the EU's normative power is Russia (Lehne,

2014). Russia perceives the Eastern Partnership as a threat to its influence in the shared neighbourhood, and thus it promotes a different set of national, cultural and religious values to the countries that it considers to belong to its sphere of influence (Babayan, 2015; Cooley, 2015). Overall this underlines the significance of external actors in the determination of local conditions and the considerations of national elites, more of which is discussed in chapter 6.

In sum, placing EU policies within a framework relying predominantly on the EU's values risks omitting or disregarding local values and could potentially disrupt the basis for the strong partnerships that the EU increasingly emphasises. Furthermore, the literature shows that the language the EU uses in its policy documents specifically to frame the basis for its partnerships with the ENP countries matters, as values are subject to interpretation. The projection of the EU as an actor representing a set of 'common' or 'universal' values is challenged because different member states have different values and priorities. Lastly, the EU has not paid sufficient attention to the environment in which it has exercised its normative power, an observation coinciding with comments made by several other scholars on the need for the EU to take into account local, national and regional conditions.

4.6 Conclusion

There is a consensus in the literature that the ENP lacks consideration for local needs and conditions. It is also debatable to what extent the ENP allows for shared or joint ownership while keeping a focus on both positive and negative conditionality. Nevertheless, it is clear that with regard to political as well as economic reforms, liberalisation and democratisation, more differentiation is needed to reflect the diverse nature of local conditions and experiences of the neighbourhood. High politics, such as national security and migration, will most likely continue to define the agenda for the EU's relationship with the neighbourhood countries. If the ENP is to achieve its aims in regional development and democratisation, then an appreciation of local experiences and perspectives is needed to shape a successful policy that works for the ENP countries as much as it does for the EU.

In terms of joint ownership and building stronger partnerships with the ENP countries, the literature clearly shows that the EU's approach to ownership needs significant improvement. A lack of clear conceptualisation of pivotal terms like 'partnership' and 'ownership' fundamentally hinder successful implementation of strategies that do embed a more balanced approach to the formulation and development of benchmarks and common initiatives under the ENP.

The literature, however, is not conclusive on whether the disregard for local conditions is driven by a lack of understanding for these conditions or rather a strategic prioritisation of the EU's own interests and perspectives. It is also not clear to what extent it is feasible to suggest that the EU will find a way to direct the ENP towards the needs of local communities and civil society in an environment increasingly defined by domestic security concerns triggered by instability and the migration crisis, especially in the MENA region. There is nonetheless a consensus in the literature that such a transition will be needed to incentivise further political reforms and contribute to democratisation in the neighbourhood.

While the literature largely argues that the ENP should include further differentiation and consideration of local conditions, not many authors present specific case studies that would demonstrate the impact of policies that lack sufficient differentiation. Some studies incorporate data from interviews and surveys with local stakeholders. Yet there is a need for serious and detailed mapping of local needs of the ENP countries.

5. PERCEPTION AND VISIBILITY

Perceptions of the ENP differ within and outside the EU. In fact, the ENP does not meet the expectations of the eastern and southern neighbours. This dissatisfaction is exacerbated by ineffective communication to citizens of the neighbourhood countries about the ENP and the EU in general. The EU's funded projects and assistance equally suffer from a lack of visibility.

5.1 Views from the EU

When reflecting on the EU's reaction to the Arab Spring, Schumacher (2011: 117) notes that "the EU has sent many rather mixed messages to various regimes (...), ranging from praise and support to outright condemnation of the different regimes' responses to growing public demands for greater political, economic and social rights". What is more, when "the EU [did] sen[d] one message and spoke with one voice" it still "pursued conflicting goals" (Börzel and Van Hüllen, 2014: 1030). The communication of these goals and the perceptions about them in the partner countries can have a heavy impact on the relationship between the EU and the ENP partner countries. Several authors assess the degree to which the EU has been (and is) coherent in promoting its values to the ENP countries, and examine how these values have been perceived, received and implemented by partner countries (Poli, 2016; Ghazaryan, 2014). For instance, based on her analysis of the main policy documents of the ENP, Ghazaryan (2014: 23) states that their language and rhetoric has produced overall ambiguity regarding both the general aims of the ENP and the suitability of the instruments selected to reach them:

> Is the ENP about preventing the emergence of new dividing lines in the European neighbourhood or is this a secondary objective? Or is it about creating 'good' neighbours who share the values of the EU, as well as its

laws and regulations in economic and social areas which would promote prosperity and security in the neighbourhood?

The issue of coherence is discussed more extensively in chapter 7 of this report.

One of the reasons accounting for such ambiguity is the different attitudes of the EU member states towards the ENP. According to Cohen-Hadria (2016: 44-45), some experts and officials argue that the member states feel disengaged from the ENP because they do not have full access to some of the ENP-related meetings (closed sessions of the Association Councils, for instance), and find the overall ENP procedures too heavy and "overwhelming", and because the EEAS plays a decisive role in the policy implementation. But it should also be underlined that the member states themselves are reluctant to be more involved in the multilateral framework and prefer to engage with ENP partners bilaterally, particularly with respect to the southern neighbourhood (Leigh, 2015; Cohen-Hadria, 2016).

What is more, there are divisions of labour between the EU and member states, but also among member states. One of these divisions becomes apparent on the issue of human rights: the member states leave to the EU the responsibility to carry difficult messages on human rights violations to the ENP states but avoid being in line with the EU statements while conducting bilateral relations with those partners (Witney and Dworkin, 2012; Biscop et al., 2012; Lehne, 2014). Such discrepancies can be especially observed in relation to the Mediterranean EU member states, while the northern countries are more eager to follow the 'more-for-more' principle (Cohen-Hadria, 2016: 45).

Another division is based on geography: the EU's Mediterranean members are more interested in the southern dimension of the ENP, while the eastern member states are more inclined to cooperate with the EU's eastern partners. As an illustration, in most cases the respective ministers from the EU attend the respective Association Councils. Such an approach provokes criticism within the EU. As one respondent from Sweden commented in the IEMed survey, "France is not the country to run EU–Algeria policy and neither should Germany, Sweden or Poland run the Union's Russia policy" (Cohen-Hadria, 2016: 45).

Consequently, along with the lack of coordination among the 28 member states, such substantive divisions between EU capitals on the policies for the southern neighbourhood considerably undermine not only ENP coherence, but also result in its lack of visibility. Another respondent to the ENP survey noted that:

> the EU at the moment is practically invisible from the South. There is still a lot to be done on the EU's side to have a joint view on questions and represent them. I don't see this happening in the short term on most of the issues, e.g. speaking with one voice on the migration issue has been impossible so far (Cohen-Hadria, 2016: 45).

In this respect, more attention has been paid recently to the EU member states' attitudes towards the ENP, particularly its eastern dimension (which may be explained by Russia's assertive policies in the region). For instance, in their analysis of the EU's reaction to the Euromaidan protests in Ukraine, Parkes and Sobják (2014) investigate how the crisis changed the member states' positions regarding its eastern neighbours. The experts argue that before the crisis erupted there were several clusters of member states based on their perceptions of the EaP. First, the cluster of Mediterranean states led by France considered Ukraine through the prism of the southern neighbourhood. Ukraine was perceived as part of the instability belt, with small to no prospect of EU membership, and which would probably follow the MENA countries' path of choppy democratic transition. The given group of states was ready to be involved in Ukraine only if that would help to upgrade the EU's policies on the southern dimension. The second cluster comprised the Benelux states, Germany and its eastern neighbours, which followed Berlin's approach towards international relations as those between regional hegemons (Russia vs Germany) that operate in a multipolar world. In this respect, Germany aimed to reduce the perception of Russia as a threat by engaging it in different ways, particularly through economic cooperation and trade (Ostpolitik). The third cluster, which included 'Anglosphere' countries like the UK, Ireland, the Netherlands and some of the Nordic states, considered the Eastern Partnership though through the prism of economic relations and the opportunity to enlarge the EU market. The last cluster of Nordic, Baltic and eastern countries around Poland and Sweden, all advocates of the EaP, viewed Ukraine as a state treading the path of the 1990s democratic transitions, while the EaP was a focus of value-based (in contrast to mercantilist) transformative influence of the West (Parkes and Sobják, 2014: 7). The authors emphasise that this classification is rather simplified because each cluster was much less homogeneous.

In this respect, it is interesting to see how the Mediterranean EU countries and the eastern members evaluate cooperation with the eastern partners and the southern neighbourhood respectively. For instance, according to Franceson (2015), despite the fact that the refugee crisis and other issues related to the southern neighbourhood are top priorities for the Italian government, the EaP is also present on its agenda. Its EaP share constitutes a third of Italy's ENP budget to spend in 2014–20. Also, Italy is Ukraine's third most important economic partner among the EU members and is an important commercial partner of Belarus. Italy is advocating a more open EU policy towards Belarus, and while supporting the EU's stance on the crisis in Ukraine, considers its policy towards Ukraine through the prism of relations with Russia, being in favour of an 'open door' policy towards the latter. Moreover, Italy has strong economic ties with Azerbaijan in such spheres as energy, environment, infrastructure and health technologies (Franceson, 2015: 6-10).

The dedication to the EaP is even less evident in the case of France. While generally supportive of the initiative by Poland and Sweden, Paris looked at relations with the eastern neighbours while taking into account Russia's position. It preferred to deal directly with Moscow rather than with EaP capitals. This was apparent during the 2008 Russia–Georgia war, when France chaired the EU presidency. As the main mediator, President Sarkozy was keen to normalise relations with Moscow just a couple of months after the conflict and strike a controversial deal on the delivery of two Mistral warships to Russia. As Nougayrede (2015: 11-13) argues, France's reluctance to become actively involved in the EaP is also conditioned by its political and economic competition in Europe with Germany, which Paris considers a lobbyist for an eastern dimension that pursues its own commercial interests. The war in Ukraine has mobilised Paris to look again in the eastern direction, although it is unclear whether France is going to change its priorities

(Nougayrede, 2015). Yet France has always actively developed relations with the southern neighbours, especially in the wake of the November 2015 terrorist attacks in Paris.

Whereas France and Italy's focus is on the southern neighbourhood, Poland considers the EaP to be its flagship project and is an advocate of the 'European aspirations' of its members. Poland is highly defensive when it comes to the accusation of the EaP and the EU in general being the reason for the ongoing conflict between Ukraine and Russia. At the same time, in recent years Poland has paid more attention to the southern neighbourhood. Still, it does recognise the qualitative difference between the latter and the eastern dimension of the ENP, i.e. the theoretical perspective of EU membership pursuant to Art. 49 TEU. Hence, Poland is in favour of a differentiated, flexible, tailor-made approach by the ENP (Buras, 2015: 30-33).

It is worth noting that following the Arab Spring, all Visegrad Four (V4) countries – Poland, Slovakia, the Czech Republic and Hungary – have been engaged, though to a different extent, in supporting post-revolutionary societies. They are suitable candidates for this task given their own political transition experience, as well as the absence of the negative imperial image in the region (Shepherd et al., 2013). Hungary, having held the EU's rotating presidency in the first half of 2011, has committed mainly politically, though substantially, while executing a task of representing the EU often on the ground. Also, Budapest was behind the reformation of the 'Community of Democracies', a coalition of countries that supported democracy promotion globally. The latter was particularly used by Slovakia as an instrument to assist reforms in such sectors as security, public administration, the judiciary, regional governance and development, and strengthening civil society. Slovakia and the Netherlands co-chaired the first EU–Tunisia task force in Tunis, uniting 17 other countries and a number of international organisations. The Czech Republic's involvement has been the least noticeable among the V4 group: it has mainly been active in the humanitarian sector and providing civil society training courses in Egypt, Libya, Tunisia and Syria. Poland, which took the rotating presidency after the Czech Republic, used this opportunity to improve its image and the visibility of V4 states in the region and the EU. Despite the fact that Warsaw did not contribute to the military operation in Libya, its foreign minister was the first minister from the EU who visited the opposition's capital Benghazi. Poland runs 30+ projects of 'track two' diplomacy in Egypt and Libya. Nevertheless, in its activities it has mainly focused on Tunisia, where it has created a Polish–Tunisian Institute of Diplomacy. Finally, the Arab Spring gave a push to the Polish idea of creating the European Endowment for Democracy (Shepherd et al., 2013)

What should be noted in terms of the eastern dimension of the ENP, despite the image of countries that are the staunchest advocates of the EaP, is that the V4 have different positions on a number of issues. After Poland, the Czech Republic is the country that concentrates most on democracy promotion in Eastern Europe, while Slovakia and Hungary tend to focus more on the Western Balkans. Hungary prioritises such issues as energy, the economy and Hungarian minority rights in its relations with neighbours (particularly in Ukraine and Moldova), while Slovakia – the most energy-dependent V4 country – has been pursuing a 'Russia first' policy, even if it is less evident now. Slovakia has become more actively involved in Moldova and, particularly, Ukraine. For example, it initiated a gathering of the Group of Friends of Ukraine back in 2013, but also started to reverse Russian gas to Ukraine in 2014. Similarly, the Czech Republic takes a more pragmatic stance on its relations with Russia (Kałan, 2013; Dostál et al., 2015). But according to Kałan (2013: 6-7), there is a lack of coordination and common strategy among the V4 on aid and civil support given to the EaP countries, while the interests of the V4 are quite selective, with too little attention given to the South Caucasus. Meanwhile, the Russia–Ukraine conflict has divided the four countries in terms of both common actions and assessment of the crisis: Poland has taken a hawkish position, while other states, especially Hungary, have criticised the EU's sanctions against Russia (Dostál et al., 2015: 16).

In sum, it could be argued that the ambiguity of the ENP's objectives might be explained by different perceptions of the ENP among the EU member states. The majority still prefers to build their relations with the ENP countries through a bilateral track rather than use the multilateral umbrella of the ENP. Despite the member states' efforts to balance normative and strategic components in their policies towards the neighbourhood, the latter is prevailing. In many cases geographical proximity and national interests are the factors that determine the level of involvement of certain member states in the southern or eastern dimensions of the neighbourhood.

5.2 Views from the neighbourhood

According to Keukeleire (2015), to get a complete understanding of the EU's relationship with and policies towards its neighbours, it is crucial to complement an EU-centred point of view with an 'outside-in' perspective. Keukeleire (2015: 227) further clarifies that "an 'outside-in' perspective means that the analyst or practitioner (diplomat or civil servant) does not take the EU's policy towards a third country or region as the only point of reference, but also tries to look at this EU policy from the perspective of the third countries or regions concerned". In this respect, in his study on external perceptions of the EU, Larsen (2014) argues that the EU is perceived by external actors chiefly as an economic power rather than a normative one. The researcher found these perceptions to be manifested in three ways:

> The first presents the EU as a partner with no special normative status. The second sees the EU as a self-declared promoter of legitimate norms, but views this as an attempt by the EU and its former colonial powers to reintroduce neo-colonial control. A third sees the EU as a power that attempts to further its own norms rather than universal norms. In the three readings, the EU does not have a special status through its norms which might give it influence (Larsen, 2014: 906).

Nevertheless, according to Larsen, the perception of the EU as a normative power is much more prominent among its eastern and southern neighbours than in the rest of the world (Larsen, 2014).

One could argue that this situation might change, however, as further discrepancies could arise between the EU portraying itself (and being perceived) as a normative actor emphasising the promotion of democratisation and the rule of law, while basing its actions and policies on different priorities and interests (Zajac,

2015). Accordingly, this accounts for possible ambiguities in the perception of what constitutes the 'European interest', which can also be affected by the language used by the EU describing requirements to partner countries under the ENP (Harpaz, 2014). Given the stress placed by the EU on democratisation, but also its apparent prioritisation of security-related issues, it would be beneficial to draw a clear image of what the broad interest and convergence is between those two objectives, something that the EU has failed to do in the past (Wetzel and Orbie, 2012).

Moreover, the institutional structure of the EU itself adds to the ambiguous perception of the ENP. For example, researchers point out that there is "no shared understanding among stakeholders outside or within the EEAS on the role, mandate and position of the Service within the EU external action architecture" (Wouters et al., 2013: 10), which causes confusion among the ENP partners about the roles and responsibilities of individual EU actors. As Wolczuk (2011) argues, institutional uncertainty during the extended formation of the EEAS as well as an inadequate amount of manpower dedicated to the EaP significantly impeded its implementation. The overall institutional complexity of the implementation of a partnership that is handled by the EEAS, DG NEAR and DG DEVCO makes the operation of multilateral platforms complicated, which in turn leads to their limited responsiveness to the needs of partner states.

A substantial part of the literature addresses the question of visibility and perceptions of the ENP in relation to the southern neighbourhood and the democratisation process in the southern ENP countries (Cadier, 2013; Dennison and Dworkin, 2011; Balfour, 2012b). Although the rapid EU response and its Joint Communication during the Arab Spring has, according to some sources, been a demonstration of coherent and successful policy formulation (Wouters, 2013), according to others the EU has prioritised its self-interests at the expense of normative principles. Such an approach raises suspicions about the EU's intentions, capabilities and commitment to democratisation beyond its borders (Hollis, 2012; Pech, 2012). For example, one of the researches on the perception of the ENP in Lebanon states that, despite an overall positive image of the ENP among academics and activists, there is growing concern regarding the recent trend in which human rights conditionality becomes a hostage of the EU interest in stability. More specifically, experts underline that the EU should be more selective in its support for Lebanon's security sector, because some of the relevant departments are responsible for human rights violations (for example, torture) (Scheller et al., 2016).

The level of EU attractiveness in the southern neighbourhood differs in each country. For example, in one of the most progressive EU partners, Tunisia, the EU did not have a positive image immediately after the uprising in light of the history of cooperation with Ben Ali's regime and the rather slow reaction (and even resistance) to the revolution (Dennison and Dworkin, 2011: 6). Yet, according to Freyburg and Richter (2015), the situation has improved since the *ancien régime* was toppled. The researchers refer to results of the EU Neighbourhood Barometer showing that more than a half of Tunisians had a "very positive" and "fairly positive" image of the EU in 2012–14, while nowadays, according to the PEW Global Attitudes survey, the trust of Tunisians in the EU is the highest among all other foreign actors (Freyburg and Richter, 2015: 12).

One observes a different picture when analysing Israel's attitudes towards the EU. According to Hollis (2012), Israel initially perceived the ENP as a definitely beneficial tool that provided it with access to the European market and the opportunity to cooperate in areas of scientific research. However, according to the recent Euromed survey, in 2015 43% of Israeli respondents, representing both governmental institutions and civil society, doubted the need to further maintain the ENP, thus making Israel (along with Turkey's 40%) the most critical ENP partner (IEMed, 2016). One should note that such perceptions correspond to the general attitudes of Israelis towards the EU. Based on various public opinion surveys and by using methods of content and discourse analysis, Pardo (2014) defines three major contradictory perceptions of the EU within Israeli society: 1) good relations with the EU are not vital for Israel; 2) Israel should join the EU as it represents a hospitable environment; and 3) the EU has an anti-Israeli attitude and the EU's geostrategic views damage Israel's security. Furthermore, the Israeli printed media depict the EU as a "political power of weakness and as a passive and failed economic actor" (Pardo, 2014: 192-193).

Similarly, according to the literature, the clear formulation and communication of values, interests and policies has been a challenge for the EU in the neighbourhood, particularly in its eastern dimension. A survey conducted with local stakeholders in the countries of the EaP has revealed that a lack of "clear aims and expectations" constitutes one of the main obstacles perceived by stakeholders concerning the effectiveness of the EaP (Dostál et al., 2015: 12). Furthermore, "disregard for country-specific factors" was also quoted among the chief concerns, especially by respondents from Belarus, Moldova and Ukraine.

Therefore, much more attention should be paid to the interests of the main actors in the EaP countries, both the elites and societies. The EU established the ENP and then the EaP to promote political and economic reforms in the neighbourhood through convergence where the primary instrument was the *acquis* as a model for positive changes. Yet, the EaP political elites did not fully embrace these objectives. According to researchers, the local elites have been pursuing several goals while engaging with European partners within the EaP framework. First, the EU has been used to achieve their geopolitical (foreign policy) goals. Second, the EU has been viewed as a source of financial support not only for their states, but also for personal gain. Third, the contacts with the EU have been used to improve their own political image and position, domestically and internationally. Fourth, cooperation with the EU could be used for regime legitimisation if the regimes were recognised as non-democratic (Wolczuk, 2011; Sadowski, 2013). Consequently, given the oligarchic nature of the majority of the EaP political regimes, the aims and interest of elites (preserving their own economic and political power) play a decisive role in defining the scope for EU cooperation with a particular EaP country. Meanwhile, in light of both the opportunities (market access) and challenges (competition) that cooperation with the EU brings in terms of the economy, local stakeholders lack a consistent position on the prospects for European integration (Sadowski, 2013: 34). Hence, the EU should take into account the interests of local actors when implementing the EaP.

In this respect, assessing the capabilities-expectations gap helps in understanding the visibility and perceptions of the ENP in the partner countries. It captures the role that the EU has in a given setting, reflecting its capabilities and the expectations about what the EU's role should be in shaping the relationship with the partner countries of the ENP (Nielsen, 2013). The capabilities-expectations gap theory has also shed light on the effectiveness of EU conditionality. As Cadier (2013) argues, the effectiveness of the EU's conditionality within the framework of the ENP can be significantly hindered by a failed convergence of the EU's policies and the expectations that partner countries attach to it. Especially in the case of the southern neighbourhood, formulating the incentives under the ENP to support democratisation and political reforms in the partner countries is crucial. For example, as Harpaz (2014) argues, the 2003 ENP promise of a possibility of "sharing everything with the Union but institutions", which was supported by a new differentiated principle, was not fully met. While the non-EU Mediterranean countries were supposed to be treated according to their needs and objectives, the action plans were "differentiated in terms of then specific details of the reforms requested, yet they constitute a low-reward, one-size-fits-all offer, which either deters most countries from implementing reform (if its requirements are too high), or induces reform-minded countries to under-deliver (if it is too low)" (Bodenstein and Furness, 2009: 392–394, 396; see also Harpaz, 2014: 439).

The relevance of taking into account the capabilities-expectations gap is also confirmed by the 2015 Euromed survey: two-thirds of its respondents think that the ENP has significantly fallen short of expectations, while 76% of respondents from Maghreb believe that "falling short of expectations leads to decreased credibility" (Balfour, 2016: 23). At the same time, Balfour notes that sometimes expectations of the ENP are unreasonably overstated, as they do not directly correspond to its tasks. For example, the majority of respondents identify the inability of the ENP to adequately respond to the Libyan and Syrian wars as one of its failures (Balfour, 2016).

Also, one should take into account the desires of autocratic leaders when analysing successes/failures of the ENP in the southern neighbourhood. In particular, according to Hollis (2012), the general public of Arab countries did not feel a lot of enthusiasm towards the ENP as a Western initiative because of the negative perception of the American interventionism (Iraq war), with which

Europeans were (rightfully or not) associated as well. Instead, the Arab regimes and their authoritarian leaders were the ones who decided to join the Partnership as it has promised them access to the large European market as well as aid (Hollis, 2012: 85-86).

Another considerable issue in terms of expectations is a membership prospect. As Kochenov and Basheska (2015) note, the ENP is completely decoupled from eventual accession prospects, which is regarded as a drawback for many eastern neighbours (although southern partners did not have such expectations from the very beginning). Still, according to the researchers, the ENP's vagueness (and Art. 49 of the TEU) allows some of the states — Ukraine, Moldova and Georgia — to consider the successful implementation of the ENP as the first required step towards a membership prospect (Kochenov and Basheska, 2015). Such a demand increases, and is just, given the fact that there is an imbalance for the three countries between the costs and benefits of implementing an association agreement and DCFTA (Leigh, 2015). As Leigh states, "it was not wise to present Ukraine with an exceedingly demanding DCFTA that required it to adopt a large part of the EU's laws, rules and standards (the *acquis*) without the prospect of membership" (Leigh, 2015: 220-221). This point is reiterated by the majority of experts, civil servants and business representatives from the EaP region. According to a survey conducted by a coalition of think tanks from the V4 countries, 91.1% of respondents from EaP countries, as well as 82.2% of surveyed V4 representatives believe that the carrot of membership would inspire further reforms (Dostál et al., 2015: 13). At the same time, Soimu et al. (2012) hold that many aspects of the ENP are perceived and understood differently not only between the partners and the EU but also among the partner countries.

For instance, according to the Euromed survey, only 37% of respondents from southern Mediterranean ENP countries favour preserving a formal distinction between the ENP's eastern and southern dimensions while such a distinction is supported by almost 60% of those surveyed from EU member states. Schumacher (2016b) finds such results rather striking because it means that the southern partners perceive themselves as being discriminated against compared with their eastern counterparts. According to the scholar, such sentiment might be explained by the idea that better geographical proximity of the eastern partners towards the EU puts them in a more favourable position compared with the EU's southern neighbours (Schumacher, 2016b: 39).

When it comes to the EaP states, there are numerous positive effects shared by members of the Partnership: the opportunity for closer political cooperation and deeper integration with the Union's members, and economic development. Also, the EaP stakeholders value the strengthening of democracy, good governance, the rule of law and the support of mobility (Dostál et al., 2015). Visa liberalisation is considered one of the most effective instruments, providing citizens with a concrete benefit of approximation with the EU (Kirova and Freizer, 2015). The EaP's most significant achievement, however, has been its contribution to the emergence of a pro-democratic, pro-European civil society, by providing financial support along with a legal and political framework for keeping governments accountable (Kirova and Freizer, 2015: 16).

Nevertheless, each country has its own specific issues with and assessments of the EaP. Armenian experts, for example, argue that there was incomplete investment in civil society as a partner for reforms (Giragosian, 2015b). Also, the EU did not have a clear and effective communication strategy to explain the benefits of the approximation with the EU to citizens of this Southern Caucasian country. Consequently, it worked for Russia's benefit, which played a security card and thus provided more reasons for Armenian society follow their government's decision to refuse to sign the association agreement and instead join the Russian-led Customs Union (Giragosian, 2015a; Navasardian, 2015). Navasardian argues that the more-for-more principle worked in Armenia during the association agreement negotiations of 2011–13 (Navasardian, 2015: 7). In contrast, Kirova and Freizer (2015) do not completely agree with this statement and argue that Armenia failed to introduce changes in many fields (anti-discrimination legislation was not passed, nor was a long-promised domestic violence law), while the EU kept delivering more-for-more assistance in spite of Armenia's pretence. As a result, experts point to the need to configure a new set of bilateral relations between the EU and Armenia, build a common EaP identity (by improving differentiation between EaP states), and pay additional attention to Russia's policies in the neighbourhood. Finally, Armenia views the EU as a mediator in negotiations with Turkey and a partner in de-escalation of the conflict with Azerbaijan (Navasardian, 2015).

The EU's insufficient involvement in the settlement of the Nagorno–Karabakh conflict does not contribute to the perception of the EU, by both Armenia and Azerbaijan, as an effective and attractive political actor (Sadowski, 2013; Alieva, 2015b). As Alieva (2015a) argues, the EU should use the Common Security and Defence Policy (CSDP) and CFSP instruments more actively in managing conflicts within the EaP. Alieva (2015a) also argues that the EU should pay more attention to the multilateral initiatives of the EaP states (GUAM, for example) in order to facilitate harmonisation of their security and economic interests, and as a way to develop a common ENP vision towards Russia. However, according to the researchers, one of the biggest problems inherent in the EU policy towards Azerbaijan is failure to take into account local structural factors (the legacy of Soviet bureaucracy and the boom in oil revenues) as well as the Azeri leadership's preference for energy and economic cooperation over that in the field of democracy and human rights (Alieva, 2015a; Alieva, 2015b; Hasanov, 2015). Thus, the more-for-more principle did not work in Azerbaijan, which showed reluctance to proceed with an association agreement and opted for negotiation on the Strategic Modernisation Partnership agreement instead (Alieva, 2015b). The EU's interest in energy cooperation with Azerbaijan resulted in downgrading its reform agenda for this country. What is more, the EU has been criticised for the lack of any tangible support for Azeri civil society and democratic institutions. According to Hasanov, "the EU has not been sincere with Azerbaijan regarding democratisation, corruption, market liberalisation and the environment", while the absence of any significant action "makes Azerbaijani society wonder about 'European values'" (Hasanov, 2015: 11).

In the case of Belarus, the EaP remains a conventional and, what is important, a sole platform for cooperation with the EU on a bilateral level, though the current level of relations between the two actors is the lowest compared with other EaP countries (Sivitski, 2015). The difficulty for EU policies lies in the absence of domestic actors (at both the governmental and societal levels, as the opposition is suppressed) that could be Europe's partners in pushing for necessary reforms (Preiherman, 2015). Thus, the more-for-more principle does not apply to the Belarusian case either. In addition, owing to the ongoing Russian–Ukrainian conflict, President Alexander Lukashenko's policy of balancing between the EU and Russia is an ever-more complicated task. Hence, the Belarusian experts advise focusing cooperation on those fields that do not challenge the current status quo within the country and will be tolerated by Russia (Sivitski, 2015; Preiherman, 2015; Halubnichy, 2015; Korosteleva, 2016c). These may include investments in a key economic sectors, deepening economic ties, technical and financial assistance for industrial modernisation, cooperation in transport and logistical projects, medicine, environmental protection and developing people-to-people contacts.

According to a study in conjunction with public opinion polls and focus groups conducted by Korosteleva (2016c), "a more tailored and low-key technical engagement is more effective and preferable, especially if it is on a continuous basis, as it has a far greater socialising effect" (Korosteleva, 2016c: 10). As the scholar notes, such cooperation is already taking place. There are 59 ongoing projects, with over 150 having been successfully completed in the past ten years under the EaP framework in Belarus. There is a twofold increase of interest in EU affairs (65%, representing a 25% increase since 2009) and Belarus–EU relations (70%, a 22% increase), while at least two-thirds of respondents state that they are familiar with the EaP initiative and more than a half of those surveyed consider relations with the EU to be very positive. It is worth noting that citizens view EU–Belarus interests as converging mainly in the areas of economic development, security and the international legal order, whereas "in relation to the [Eurasian Economic Union] or Belarus, respondents do not seem to refer to 'democracy' as a value at all, but instead prioritise stability, security and cultural tradition" (Korosteleva, 2016c: 6). Thus, Koroseteleva (2016c: 2) emphasises that Belarus, similar to the post-Soviet space, is normatively different to the EU. Moreover, it is also "increasingly self-conscious and protective of its own identity". The EU's naming-and-shaming approach might not be beneficial to the situation in Belarus. Another important point to take into account is that Belarusian citizens do not regard the EU and the Eurasian Economic Union (EAEU) as complementary projects, but rather see them as overlapping and dichotomous. Consequently, some scholars argue that the EU should find a way to cooperate with the EAEU for the sake of stability in Belarus and the eastern neighbourhood in general (Korosteleva, 2016c; Preiherman, 2015). Such emphasis on the need for cooperation with the EAEU is also evident in the case of Armenia.

In a nutshell, perception of the ENP by the EU's partners in the south and east varies and depends on the interest of neighbours. Yet, there is a consensus among ENP societies regarding the EU as an actor that fails to meet its partners' expectations, be they on security provision, economic cooperation or political support. What is more, despite the many benefits the ENP provides to their societies, the neighbours perceive the ENP as a tool to pursue the pragmatic interests of EU member states at the expense of a commitment to promote EU values abroad.

5.3 Visibility and communication strategies

In his comprehensive study of the EU's support for Ukraine, Gressel states that the EU is losing in the area of visibility and communication to the main national (the US and Japan) and international donors. More specifically, the EU outsources its assistance to other aid agencies when it deals with humanitarian assistance and does not have much responsibility for day-to-day communication with people in need on the ground. As a result, the population is not aware of the kind or magnitude of support from the EU and its member states. One of the exceptions mentioned by the author is the German development agency GIZ, which has a wide network of staff who are quite flexible in their response to the immediate needs of internally displaced persons (Gressel, 2016: 63).

Moreover, according to a representative survey, Ukrainian citizens in general do not have a clear position regarding EU assistance to their country. The average score given to the EU by respondents was 5.36 (on a scale of 1 to 10), as the lowest, middle and highest scores were given in almost equal number by those interviewed. Importantly, the financial support by the EU was ranked 11th on the list of important measures expected from the EU, while Ukrainian citizens favoured greater involvement of the EU in domestic politics (the top choice at 30.12%, as ranked by respondents) (Solodkyy and Sharlay, 2015: 17-18). In the same vein, Kirova and Freizer (2015: 16) argue that the EaP has two failings: it has not taken into account the public's perceptions and some of its policies are significantly misunderstood. For example, the researchers cite data from surveys conducted in the EaP: the EU enjoyed highly positive attitudes among Georgians (58%) and Ukrainians (56%), but much less among Azeris (28%). Other polls, mentioned by Kirova and Freizer (2015), have also shown a high degree of support for the EU: 85% in Georgia and a rise from 47 to 56% in Ukraine in 2014. Still, these high levels of support do not automatically lead to a better understanding of the opportunities that closer integration brings. For instance, according to the results of a 2013 survey, Georgian citizens were largely under-informed about the EU, while only 23% said they had heard of the EaP. In Moldova, after the EU–Moldova Association Agreement was signed, 60% stated that they were poorly or not at all informed about the agreement.

At the same time, as mentioned earlier, one could observe an improvement in the EU's image as a partner contributing to development among the populations of the eastern neighbourhood states. According to EU Neighbourhood Barometer data, it rose from 38% in 2013 to 44% in 2014. Thus, as Kimber and Halliste (2015) argue in their study, the EU should seize the opportunity given by the current trend and invest more in boosting its image. In this regard, they identify common issues the EaP countries have to tackle while trying to foster effective EU-related communication. For example, the authors mention such challenges as adjusting to the new realm of communication (the need for creative messages targeted at specific groups), underestimating the importance of EU-related communication, implementing communication strategies that are usually left on paper, poorly locating communication units within organisational structures and the proliferation of technical jargon in communications (Kimber and Halliste, 2015: 25-27). The authors offer a set of recommendations for actors in EaP states and the EU institutions on how to improve EU-related communication on the ground.

Additionally, Kimber and Halliste (2015: 32-34) recommend that the EU hire communication professionals instead of relying on general members of staff and update the communication and visibility manual for EU external actions introduced back in 2010. Their recommendations also include providing visual coverage of the work of the project teams on the ground rather than photos from official meetings, producing EU information materials that are suitable for the local population (highlighting language, simple and short messages and leaflets instead of glossy magazines). They stress the need for using 'human' language and keeping project websites lively by engaging with visitors and developing new formats for interaction among people (an "EU club"). Added to the list is involving local policy and opinion-makers in EU-related communications, conducting foreign language training for journalists, focusing on cooperation with broadcasters and TV channels, especially regarding local EU-related projects, and engaging with local journalists directly instead of sending ready-made articles.

Many of the aforementioned points are similar to another study that addresses the issue of improving communication in a specific sector – budgetary support instruments. According to the study, the given instrument of EU support is still too abstract for the population; thus the EU should concentrate on how to attract media and social attention in order to communicate the extent of the EU's financial assistance (Kaca et al., 2014: 11). The study specifically recommends that the EU delegations make regular contact with the media regarding budget-support activities, and that their main communication messages should not contain as much data on the amounts as on the positive effects that aid brings to the state and society. Convening special presentations and launch events with the participation of high-ranking national officials (the president and prime minster) and the head of the EU delegation in a particular country should also be a regular practice. Finally, all information about the process of implementing programmes should be available to the public and dispersed through regular press releases (Kaca et al., 2014: 11).

Another study on Ukraine advises using the pre-accession experience of Poland and other Central European countries when raising awareness about the EU (Skorupska, 2014). Skorupska argues that the EU's communication strategy should be adjusted to the current political situation (against the background of the military conflict and Russian propaganda), and its messages should be tailored to each specific region of Ukraine. Moreover, the issue of economics should be underlined during the campaign: examples of the current state of the economy in Central European and the Baltic states should be brought in, while also showing both the positive and negative consequences of EU membership. The researcher also recommends involving celebrities in the promotion of the EU, following the example of referendum campaigns in Poland and Croatia. It is crucial to refocus communication activities from those groups that have already been convinced of the benefits of the European path of development (e.g. experts and journalists), while using them to reach out to the wider population. When it comes to increasing visibility among the population of authoritarian states such as Azerbaijan, experts suggest that the EU ought to concentrate on areas like disabled-friendly transportation, and environmentally clean and safe construction methods (Alieva, 2015a: 17).

According to Kirova and Freizer (2015: 29), despite some improvements, the EaP's "visibility strategy" launched in 2013 to reinforce EU efforts to better explain the concrete benefits of its initiatives has not been visible on the ground. The researchers especially note that there is a lack of financial and human resources for the EU delegations, which is somewhat mitigated by the communication projects conducted by other pro-European NGOs (for example, the Open Society Foundation and its partners). Besides working with local authorities and civil society, the researchers suggest building up the capacity of EaP governments in communications. As examples they mention the financing of a strategic communications and policy planning adviser in the Moldovan prime minister's office in 2012, and the establishment of a Communication Coordination Unit on EU projects and implementation of the association agreement in Georgia (March 2015) (Kirova and Freizer, 2015: 30).

In sum, the EU lacks an effective communication strategy in its neighbourhood, consequently leading to decreasing visibility of the EU and a lack of knowledge about the ENP's objectives (and benefits) within partners' societies. To create and maintain a positive image, the EU will need to invest more human and financial resources in the development of informational networks. Also, in its communication activities the EU should try to reach a wider audience and speak with ENP societies in more understandable 'human' language.

5.4 Conclusion

According to the literature, perceptions and understanding of the objectives of the ENP on the side of the EU is ambiguous and varies depending on the interests of European capitals. The EU member states consider it a secondary policy tool, as they prefer to conduct their relations with the ENP partners through their own bilateral forms of cooperation. One could argue that there is an informal 'division of labour' within the EU, according to which the ENP is perceived as an instrument that complements the EU member states' foreign policies, particularly by being responsible for a normative part of the EU's agenda (e.g. promotion of democracy and human rights).

The perception of the ENP by the neighbourhood countries differs and depends on each country's specific priorities and expectations. In general, the ENP is perceived as an important framework for cooperation, but not capable of triggering real changes in ENP societies due to its inflexibility and technocratic character. In this respect, the EU is criticised for not taking into account the perceptions of its neighbours about the ENP while shaping its policies and for a lack of strategic visibility in the neighbourhood. It is also crucial to understand that perception is a subjective reflection by the actors involved, and thus one should not equate perception of the ENP with its objective condition. What is more, the majority of the literature tends to generalise perceptions of the EU and the ENP, while only several studies make a clear distinction between them in the actors' perceptions (EU officials vs EU national officials vs officials from ENP countries, and EU civil society representatives vs ENP civil society organisations). Also, one should take into account general public opinion both within the EU and the ENP states regarding the relations between the EU and its neighbours when analysing the issues of perception and visibility, and not only rely on officials and institutionalised civil society.

It is important to emphasise that the issue of (external) perception of the EU has gained prominence relatively recently (since the early 2000s). In this respect, the topic of the ENP constitutes only part of the general debates about the image of the Union on the global stage. Hence, it could be difficult to separate perceptions of the ENP from overall perceptions of the EU. Particularly because of the supranational nature of the ENP, much less attention has been paid to the individual member states' attitudes towards the ENP and its effectiveness. One could note that the Ukraine–Russia conflict has stimulated research in this area. However, there is still a paucity of studies on the perceptions of the ENP within and outside the EU. Notably, there is a lack of case studies on perceptions of the ENP within individual southern partners.

Finally, there is a consensus within the literature when it comes to the issue of visibility: the ENP and the EU in general lack visibility in the neighbouring countries. Reiterating the arguments presented by the literature in chapter 4, to tackle this problem the EU is advised to gather a deeper understanding of local populations' attitudes while closely cooperating with ENP stakeholders (both civil society and governments) in the process of developing communication strategies. As might be expected, EU policies in this field should be supported with sufficient financial means and human resources.

6. EXTERNAL FACTORS

The EU views the Sahel, the Gulf states, Central Asia and Russia as 'neighbours of its neighbours' (Gstöhl and Lannon, 2015). Within the framework of the ENP, the concept of neighbours of the neighbours was first introduced in 2006 by the European Commission with the aim of describing areas of potential trans-regional cooperation (Lannon, 2015). The external (f)actors considered in this report go beyond the neighbouring countries of the ENP states. These factors include not only countries like Russia in the eastern neighbourhood and Saudi Arabia and Iran in the south, but also non-state actors and drivers, like the so-called Islamic State, climate change and demographic growth, which can all significantly impact the domestic and regional dynamics in the European neighbourhood.

There are several questions that arise from consideration of the neighbours of the neighbours. The EU conducts political dialogue and maintains economic, trade and diplomatic relations with all neighbours of the neighbours, although as the literature shows, there are significant variances in the extent and nature of these relationships (Gstöhl, 2015). Relations with the countries in the wider neighbourhood have also been conducted within the framework of the CFSP through the EU special representatives (EUSRs), and the CSDP (Gstöhl, 2015; Bello, 2012; Zulaika, 2012).

In terms of formats, the EU conducts relations with the neighbours of the neighbours on a bilateral, multilateral, interregional or sub-regional level (Gstöhl, 2015). The models of cooperation differ from state to state and according to the region. As Gstöhl (2015) argues, while the EU's relations with African states take place on a multilateral and interregional level, inter-regionalism and bilateralism is more common in the Middle Eastern region and in Central Asia.

The most studied case of the neighbours of the neighbours has been the interaction between the EU and Russia in the eastern neighbourhood. As this chapter will demonstrate, the European Union has consistently struggled to define a strategy in the eastern neighbourhood that would include Russia and take into account Moscow's considerations and interests in the neighbourhood. Thus, in general, the literature explores not only the role of external actors in the ENP countries, but also how the EU can and should incorporate them into existing ENP structures and strategies.

The 6th annual Euromed survey conducted by the European Institute for the Mediterranean in 2015 revealed strong support for strengthening trans-regional cooperation in several different policy areas, including conflict resolution, regional security and law enforcement, economic and trade cooperation, education and culture, employment, humanitarian assistance and civil society (Lannon, 2015). In the most extensive publication on this topic to date, Gstöhl (2015) reiterates that a lack of cooperation with the wider regional neighbourhood is not sustainable in the long run.

6.1   Southern neighbourhood

External factors and neighbours of the neighbours play an important role in the southern neighbourhood. Apart from the influence of regional actors such as Saudi Arabia and Iran (Blockmans et al., 2016), several other external aspects accounting for different regional circumstances are relevant, including migratory flows, a growing number of conflicts and an ever-more challenging environment caused by demographic growth (Faleg and Blockmans, 2016; Kaunert and Leonard, 2011; Grevi, 2014; Kausch, 2013).

The 6th Euromed survey revealed that a significant number of respondents consider the expansion of the geographical scope of the ENP necessary, particularly in relation to the neighbours of the neighbours in the southern dimension (Lannon, 2015). More than half of the respondents recommended extending the scope of the ENP to the countries in the Sahel region. This demonstrates the strategic and geopolitical significance of these countries to the ENP, as likewise stressed in a number of studies (Mattelaer, 2015; Zulaika, 2012; Gstöhl, 2015). Accordingly, there is a consensus on the need for deepening and strengthening partnerships with the neighbours of the neighbours.

While in the case of the eastern neighbourhood Russia is certainly the most prominent external actor, the literature concerning the neighbours of the neighbours in the southern neighbourhood is more concerned with regional dynamics as a whole and how the EU's presence in the region can have an impact on the European neighbourhood. This highlights the need for coherence in ENP initiatives with wider regional strategies and policy frameworks. In this regard, the ENP has also been described, for example, as "bilateralism-within-regionalism" (Gstöhl, 2015: 283). Given the particularities of the Sahel region, such as weakness of the state structures and institutions (Mattelaer, 2015), the surrounding regions and how the EU approaches them are undoubtedly significant aspects affecting regional security and stability.

An increasing number of conflicts in the MENA region have exacerbated the risk attached to the southern dimension of the ENP. These conflicts, including the 2012–13 conflict in Mali, which has had a significant impact on the presence in the region of both the EU and the US, only add to the unstable security situation in the region, which has been characterised by prevailing polarisation partially caused by the Israeli–Palestinian conflict and other factors (Thompson, 2015; Whitman and Juncos, 2012; Bello, 2012). Terrorism, the rise of radical Islam and civil wars all constitute a major challenge for the EU's foreign policy (Henökl and Stemberger, 2016: 227-228).

Some authors view the ENP as an important tool for the fight against the terrorism (Kaunert and Léonard, 2011). In recent years the European Union has increased the level of cooperation with some of the neighbours of the neighbours specifically in the field of counter-terrorism (Bower and Metais, 2015). Other external actors present in the region, including the US, have mirrored this commitment to counter-terrorism cooperation as well (Thompson, 2015).

The rise of extremism and Islamic militant groups such as the Islamic State have had, according to some authors, a profound effect not only on the countries in which the groups directly operate, but also on the security dynamics of the wider region (Whitman and Juncos, 2012). Bello (2012), however, finds that the EU's contribution to the capacity building of the states in the region in fighting and preventing extremism is limited. The rise of various resurgent terrorist and separatist groups, especially in the Sahel, might furthermore have an impact on the efforts to establish more effective coordination among the regional powers (Bello, 2012).

Across the entire region of North Africa, high poverty rates, climate change and environmental conditions like droughts and deforestation, along with rapid demographic growth have profoundly affected the ability of the states themselves as well as external actors to maintain regional stability (Zulaika, 2012). The southern neighbours of the neighbours also play a significant role with regard to the region's energy relations and natural resources. Iraq, for example, has progressively become a more important player in the area of energy, and the Gulf countries traditionally remain the most important actors in this field due to their dominance in the oil and gas industry (Bower and Metais, 2015).

Increasing instability and insecurity in the MENA region as well as dramatic surges in migration and refugee flows have led to reviews of the ENP. At the operational level, the EU has tried to improve the management of rising migration flows through sea patrolling, burden sharing among the EU member states (Guild and Carrera, 2016) and naval force deployment to combat illegal trafficking of migrants across the Mediterranean (Faleg and Blockmans, 2016; Blockmans, 2016). The refugee crisis and growing concerns about possible additional migration and security challenges have brought the dialogue on visa facilitation to a virtual deadlock (Neuvonen, 2015). Beyond the fight against radicalisation and efforts to mitigate further migration pressures, some researchers see energy as a key area amid an effort to review Euro-Mediterranean economic cooperation at a time of economic hardship, high unemployment and difficult domestic conditions caused by the refugee crisis (Tagliapietra and Zachmann, 2016).

The literature further describes the changing geopolitical environment that is significantly affecting the presence of the EU and the effectiveness of its action in the MENA region (Kausch, 2013; Grevi, 2014; Zulaika, 2012). This environment in the southern neighbourhood has first and foremost been defined by the rise of the Islamic State in Syria and Iraq and the regional spillover effects it has produced (Whitman and Juncos, 2012). Perthes (2011) argues that to increase its leverage in the region, the EU must be able to pay attention to the region's geopolitical context next to the individual countries, as well as political and economic developments – something with which the EU has struggled.

According to Grevi (2014), the geopolitical environment of the southern neighbourhood is primarily characterised by a high level of interdependency with the wider geopolitical space stretching from West Africa, the Sahel and the Middle East up to Central Asia and Russia. Further factors contributing to the regional geopolitical dynamic is the growing sectarian rift between Sunni and Shia affiliations at both the local and national levels (Kausch, 2013).

Beyond geopolitics the EU has been working towards the development of regional economic integration as well as the strengthening of cooperation in political affairs and the establishment of regional institutions (Thompson, 2015). These efforts have to some extent been replicated in the Sahel, along the Horn of Africa and Central Asia (Thompson, 2015). The following sections reflect on the impact of global powers, regional actors and dynamics particularly in the Gulf, Sahel and Horn of Africa.

In sum, the role of external actors in the southern dimension of the ENP remains largely understudied. The literature recognises that regional actors such as Saudi Arabia, Turkey and Iran have a significant influence on regional geopolitical and security dynamics. However, in contrast to literature focusing on the eastern neighbourhood, the literature does not offer any articulate conclusions on how external actors influence, for example, sectoral convergence or democratisation in the region. Furthermore, the literature argues for the importance of trans-regional initiatives dealing with issues that require closer regional cooperation. At the same time, scholars also agree on the need to further differentiate and adapt existing frameworks to the local needs and dynamics on the ground.

6.1.1 The role of global actors

Scholars analysing the southern neighbourhood focus on the inclusion of, the role and dynamics among 'global players' in the region (Thompson, 2015; Perthes, 2011; Völkel, 2014). Despite assumptions that the US has significantly reduced its focus on the Middle East and North Africa, it continues to be perceived as an actor with a significant amount of power and leverage in the region, including ENP countries (Völkel, 2014). The involvement of the US in the southern Mediterranean has largely declined because of the attention on the Middle East, especially Israel and its immediate neighbours, the Persian Gulf and Iran (Perthes, 2011). Nevertheless, Grevi (2014: 15) argues that the regional environment in the southern neighbourhood is more challenging and volatile for the EU, given that "the United States' engagement in the region is going to become more selective and perhaps less decisive". By contrast, according to Völkel (2014), after the invasion of Iraq support for the US in the region significantly dropped, which could lead to a rise in the EU's credibility as an alternative actor, for instance in peace negotiations or crisis management situations.

The activities of the US have in recent years concentrated on the areas of security, counter-terrorism and humanitarian aid (Thompson, 2015). The US has made new commitments to region-wide reform of the security sector and military training in the Sahel and the Horn of Africa, and according to Thompson (2015), has increased efforts to strengthen region-wide intelligence gathering for support of effective counter-terrorism. Counter-terrorism was also at the centre of the US flagship Pan-Sahel Initiative in 2002. This initiative was later expanded to include some of the countries within the ENP, including Algeria and Morocco.

In general, to resolve the many conflicts that are currently afflicting the region's security and political dynamics, the literature recommends that the EU should seek to work more closely with other external actors, including the US and regional actors that are not members of the ENP (Perthes, 2011; Whitman and Juncos, 2012; Mattelaer, 2015).

Besides the US, three major Asian actors, namely China, South Korea and India, have expanded their economic and trade interests in the region, even though their links to the southern Mediterranean countries has been limited to economic ties, without paying much attention to or trying to influence political developments (Perthes, 2011). This has made the EU practically the only major actor in the region whose interests comprise security and political development, as well as economic and trade relations. Some studies nevertheless suggest that the involvement of China in the form of bilateral agreements with resource-rich countries, especially in Africa, could possibly have a deteriorating effect on regional governance and relations while "deepening regional disparities and discouraging inclusive forms of regional cooperation" (Thompson, 2015: 248).

To conclude, the changing roles of global actors, particularly China and the US, undoubtedly present an opportunity for the EU to redefine its approach to the region. The southern dimension of the ENP is one of the most important initiatives and policy instruments that the EU has at its disposal. The literature, however, lacks detail about what the EU could do to improve its standing in the region or how can the EU could make the ENP more effective in addressing the challenges of the changing environment in its southern neighbourhood.

6.1.2 Regional actors and institutions

The bulk of the literature studies the interaction between the EU and regional actors and how it impacts the EU's influence in the southern neighbourhood and the surrounding regions (Mattelaer, 2015; Perthes, 2011; Völkel, 2014, Whitman and Juncos, 2012; Bower and Metais, 2015; Rieker, 2014). As Thompson (2015) argues, there is a different level of regional integration and cooperation in the areas surrounding the southern neighbourhood states. While the states of the Sahel and the littoral Mediterranean are characterised by weak institutions and low levels of regional economic integration, some cooperation is visible, particularly in the Gulf region. Nonetheless, there are several regional actors, including Nigeria, Iran, Saudi Arabia and others, that have significantly shaped the regional political dynamics and with which the EU has engaged on a regional or bilateral level (Mattelaer, 2015; Thompson, 2015).

The literature indicates that the Gulf states can be seen as the most essential regional actors among the 'neighbours of the neighbours'. Somehow mirroring the dynamics between the European Union and the EAEU project, the decisions of some countries in the Middle East to cooperate closer with the Gulf Cooperation Council could potentially decrease their readiness to seek closer ties with the European Union (Perthes, 2011; Völkel, 2014). The appeal of economic integration with the EU might be significantly reduced by the presence of countries such as Saudi Arabia or Qatar, which can offer more unconditional financial support to some countries in the region. As Völkel (2014: 278) confirms, this is particularly relevant with regard to the EU's approach towards newer democracies in the region: "Applying too strict benchmarks to the regime's performance might push them more to donors from the Gulf."

To avoid the same kind of zero-sum dynamics that has characterised the eastern neighbourhood, Perthes (2011) argues that the EU must seek to build mutual confidence among all the actors involved in the region. Furthermore, it should try to understand precisely the kind of geopolitical and conflict dynamics that affect political developments in the countries with which it has closer ties, including mapping the geopolitical roles and interests of external actors. As the literature argues, the EU might not be considered the best-equipped actor to engage in effective conflict resolution in the given geopolitical dynamics (Whitman and Juncos, 2012). This has for instance been exemplified by the Middle Eastern peace process, in which the EU failed to engage with other regional actors and assume a leading position in the peace-building process (Whitman and Juncos, 2012).

Saudi Arabia is a major external actor influencing the effectiveness of EU policies vis-à-vis the MENA region (Rieker, 2014). According to Lannon (2015), it was primarily the events of the Arab Spring that highlighted the interconnectedness of the southern neighbourhood region with the Gulf states. Specifically, Saudi Arabia is portrayed as an influential actor opposing the democratic transition of the region following the Arab Spring, thus gaining the status of a 'counter revolutionary' actor (Hassan, 2015; Blockmans et al., 2016). Saudi Arabia has significantly increased its financial aid flows to several countries of the southern neighbourhood, including Egypt, Jordan, Tunisia and Morocco (Rieker, 2014). Furthermore, the extensive degree of economic links between the Gulf countries, specifically Saudi Arabia, Qatar and the UAE, and the southern Mediterranean, as well as the large amount of investment Gulf countries have in the region, is a particular aspect to be considered especially in relation to the EU's conditionality (Echagüe, 2012). Lastly, in recent years the Gulf countries have also significantly expanded their involvement in political affairs of the region and mediation of crises, exemplified by the crisis in Syria (Bower and Metais, 2015). This is mirrored in the strong support of Saudi Arabia, but also Qatar and Kuwait, for local and national Islamist parties such as the Egyptian Salafist An-Nur Party (Völkel, 2014).

In the Sahel, Nigeria has been one of the most important regional players. Mattelaer (2015) argues that insufficient integration of Nigeria and Mali into the regional political framework prevents effective cooperation at the regional level and therefore hinders progress on a trans-regional scale. Mali might not be an influential actor in itself but the situation in the country significantly affects the regional dynamics and the involvement of external actors, such as the EU and the US (Mattelaer, 2015; Thompson, 2015).

According to Zulaika (2012), the EU has addressed neighbours of the southern neighbourhood, including the Sahel, in two distinct ways. On the one hand, the EU has acknowledged the differences in the regional characteristics of the Sahel and the Horn of Africa. On the other hand, the EU has included both regions in an overarching political framework of the ACP group (Africa, Caribbean and Pacific countries).

In sum, scholars focusing on the role of regional actors, particularly the Gulf states, argue for a strengthened model of cooperation between the EU and the Gulf states to avoid a similar scenario to that of EU–Russia relations and the eastern neighbourhood. While the literature underscores the importance of strengthening regional cooperation, it does not elaborate much on the nature of the interests of external actors, such as Saudi Arabia and Algeria, in the region. Therefore, while potential conflicts could arise between those actors and the EU in terms of furthering the integration of ENP countries with the EU, the particular nature of this conflict is not analysed extensively.

6.2 Eastern neighbourhood

While upgrading its policies in the eastern neighbourhood, the EU effectively boosted its presence in what has been described as the 'common neighbourhood' between the EU and Russia. This is especially evident in the EU's offer of association agreements and

DCFTAs to three of the eastern neighbourhood countries within the framework of the Eastern Partnership. These agreements entail domestic change through offering hard-law integration. This has been perceived by Russia as an attempt to control what it considers its sphere of influence (Delcour and Kostanyan, 2014). In return, Russia has been said to actively strive to undermine the EU's policies vis-à-vis the eastern neighbourhood (Emerson and Kostanyan, 2013). This has been apparent since the launch of the EaP in 2009, which has accordingly sparked the reconceptualisation of Russian policy in the common neighbourhood and provided an impetus to the development of the EAEU (Sololenko and Hallgren, 2015, Blockmans et al., 2012).

The EU–Russia common neighbourhood has effectively turned into a 'contested neighbourhood'. Russian pressure on former Ukrainian President Victor Yanukovych not to sign the negotiated EU–Ukraine Association Agreement has been the most prominent example of Russia's effort to obstruct EU policies vis-à-vis the former Soviet space (Delcour et al., 2015). Under Russian pressure, Armenia abandoned the association agreement and the DCFTA that it had negotiated with the EU, opting for membership of the EAEU instead (Kostanyan, 2015).

Even if it was already present during the first term of Russian President Vladimir Putin, assertiveness in Russian foreign policy has been particularly visible during Putin's third term, with Russia paying significant attention to opposing the common neighbours' closer association with the EU and putting an emphasis on Eurasian integration (Berg, 2014; Meister, 2013). According to Liik (2014), Putin's third presidential term has been marked primarily by a general sentiment of disappointment with the West shared among many of Russia's leading elites, which contributed to a 'pivot' towards Eurasia. This process has accordingly been accompanied by the intensification of the EU's presence in the east and 'rapprochement' with the eastern neighbourhood (Fischer, 2012).

While Russia has been excluded from the framework of the ENP, by its own preference, various cooperation frameworks have been established between the EU and Russia, and resulted in the signing of the Partnership and Cooperation Agreement (PCA) and the adoption of the roadmaps relating to the 'Four Common Spaces' for cooperation in 2005 (Fischer, 2012). Despite the existence of the

PCA and the roadmaps, EU–Russia relations have continually been deteriorating, especially in the aftermath of the Russia–Georgia war in 2008 and difficulties with the re-negotiation of the PCA after its expiry in 2007 (Fischer, 2012).

As Berg (2014: 1) notes, the eastern neighbourhood has largely been perceived by the EU as a "buffer zone between internal stability and a chaotic external environment that threatens illegal immigration, organized crime, disease and poverty". By contrast, the common neighbourhood is perceived by Russia in more geopolitical terms, connected to the historical legacy of the Soviet Union. Berg (2014) argues that to the Russian Federation, the region still remains largely defined by its close cultural, ethnic and historical links to the former Soviet space and hence to Russia itself. As a consequence, Russia has previously been alleged to use legacy-based institutional and economic interdependencies to counter the diffusion of European norms and practices in the neighbourhood (Delcour, 2016a). Fischer (2012) furthermore argues that since the breakup of the Soviet Union, the Eastern European space including Russia has experienced a re-introduction and re-definition of 'Europeanness', thus introducing a clear discursive split between European 'insiders' and 'outsiders'. In Russian discourses, this period has also seen a political, economic and identity crisis as the former superpower has attempted to redefine its national and regional identity (Fischer, 2012).

Dependency on oil, gas and other natural resources from Russia has often been mentioned as an aspect contributing to Russia's relative power and leverage over the countries in the common neighbourhood. Some others recommend that the EU help the countries in the common neighbourhood on the path to less energy dependency on Russia, as a fundamental step to empowerment (Lebduška and Lidl, 2014). The conflict between the EU and Russia in Ukraine has furthermore had an impact on energy security not only in the neighbourhood but also in the EU itself, during a time in which the EU is making significant efforts towards diversification (Proedrou, 2016).

Russia undoubtedly is the most widely studied external actor with regard to the ENP. There is a significant consensus that Russia poses a challenge to the EU's role in the region. However, as the following sections demonstrate, there are varying opinions on the extent to which Russia has impacted various parts of the ENP, including sectoral convergence and security cooperation.

6.2.1 Differing paths of integration

Membership of the Commonwealth of Independent States (CIS) has also constituted a factor pertaining to close relations between Russia and the countries in the post-Soviet space (Lebduška and Lidl, 2014). A 'Russkiy mir' concept describing the common space uniting all countries with a 'Soviet legacy' and cultural ties to Russia has also often been cited in Russian political discourse justifying, for example, the intervention in Ukraine. According to Lebduška and Lidl (2014), however, in the last few years the Russian policy in the region goes directly against this principle, which seeks to unite the geopolitical space surrounding Russia under its leadership. Therefore, while some authors suggest that Russia has been the driving force behind creating a zero-sum game environment in the eastern neighbourhood, Delcour (2016a) argues that Moscow has perceived instruments such as the EaP and the DCFTAs as modelled to make the EaP countries choose between either integration with the EU or continuing close relations within the CIS framework.

Even though the countries of the EaP are allowed to enter into free trade agreements with both the European Union and the Russian Federation, membership of the Russia-led EAEU is not compatible with the EU's DCFTA (Emerson and Kostanyan, 2013; Dragneva and Wolczuk, 2014, Ademmer et al., 2016). Likewise, former European Commissioner Stefan Füle confirmed this assumption, announcing that the association agreement with Armenia would not be completed if the Armenian authorities decided to join the Russian-backed Customs Union project (Wisniewski, 2013).

In Russia itself, the European Union and the ENP have mostly been perceived as hindering further cooperation between Russia and the neighbourhood countries, particularly economic and trade cooperation (Zagorski, 2011; Sadowski, 2013). The integration with the EU is therefore seen as going hand in hand with a gradual disintegration of relations with Russia. This consideration is not limited to trade, but also concerns energy, transport and mobility cooperation between the EaP countries and Russia (Zagorski, 2011).

As Lebduška and Lidl (2014: 5) note, the years after the Vilnius Summit in 2014 are "characterized by the clash between European and Eurasian integration models and value systems".

An interesting dichotomy can be found in Russia's approach to the types of intergovernmental or multilateral institutions spearheaded by the EU. On the one hand, Russia has traditionally perceived multilateral and regional cooperation frameworks favoured by the EU with uncertainty and contrary to its interests, even though it does not perceive them as "an acute challenge" (Zagorski, 2011: 47). On the other hand, as demonstrated by the Eurasian Customs Union project, Russia has increasingly sought to actively work against integration with the West by providing incentives for countries in the common neighbourhood to join its own cooperation platforms (Sadowski, 2013). The incentives offered to those countries within the cooperation and institutional frameworks are often seen as more attractive since financial support is not conditioned on the achievement of political reforms or the advancement of democratisation. Considerations of the neighbourhood countries are also influenced by the fact that economic integration with the EU in the form of both association agreements and the DCFTAs are assumed to bring more structural benefits to the countries in the long term by lowering trade barriers, reducing corruption and improving both competition and foreign direct investment through comprehensive reforms of the regulatory framework (Meister, 2013).

According to Berg (2014), not only do the integration efforts pursued by both the EU and Russia increasingly alienate the two parties since they are perceived as mutually hindering, but also the strategies of integration are effectively precluding any kind of future improvement in relations between the EU and the Russian Federation. Niktina (2014) argues that the EU and Russia have traditionally pretended not to play a zero-sum game in the region. The author holds that the first step in overcoming the zero-sum mentality that has developed in the region would be mutual recognition of the aspiration of different normative goals (e.g. economic vs ideational and governance-related). Similarly, some authors have suggested that both the EU and Russia should transcend the rhetoric of a "new Cold War", and that for the EU to be a viable actor in the common neighbourhood it needs to be able to make realistic assessments of the interests and expectations that shape Russian foreign policy (Monaghan, 2015: 2; Meister, 2013). Instead of contesting one another and aiming to prevent integration of the common neighbourhood countries with the opposing party, both actors should move towards a policy of balancing (Meister, 2013). Hett et al. (2014), however, argue that the crisis in Ukraine has first and foremost demonstrated that the current environment in the eastern neighbourhood effectively eliminates the possibility for the EU to increase cooperation with the EaP countries and build a strategic partnership with Russia at the same time.

The decisions taken by individual countries can in some cases be mirrored by or actively change the position taken by other countries (Berg, 2014). In this sense, the initial decision of former President Victor Yanukovych to cancel the signing of an association deal with the EU would have significantly increased the leverage of the Russian Federation on Moldova as well. In contrast, the accession of Armenia to the Russian-backed Customs Union could incentivise a new phase in EU–Georgia relations.

Apart from questions of economic and political integration in different multilateral or bilateral platforms, several studies argue that the countries of the common neighbourhood have also been subject to hybrid warfare and the use of soft power instruments at the hands of the Kremlin with the goal of undermining the political dynamics in those countries (Meister and Puglierin, 2015; Laruelle et al., 2015). Hybrid warfare includes the use of a wide range of political, information and economic instruments, which seek to influence the events in a certain target state. Not only in relation to the common neighbourhood, but also some of the EU member states have concerns been continually raised about the extent to which Russia aims to influence public opinion and political developments. Although Russia merely claims to be using the same kind of soft power instruments in the common neighbourhood as the EU to promote democratisation and political reforms, there are worries about the nature of the techniques and the intentions behind Russia's activities in the region (Meister and Puglierin, 2015).

In sum, the extent to which Russia influences the policy choices of the EaP countries is a contentious issue in the ENP scholarship. While some authors believe that Russia has successfully discredited further integration and cooperation with the EU, others see the result as less negative for the EaP countries' relations with the EU. Scholarship focusing on geopolitics characterises the common neighbourhood as a geopolitical space that is increasingly defined by zero-sum dynamics between the EU and Russia, a dynamic that is unfavourable for the ENP countries and the EU. Naturally, the EU needs to build a closer partnership with the EaP countries and make better use of existing initiatives to prevent further deterioration of the geopolitical and security environment in the eastern ENP dimension. However, this does not provide a solution for the challenge posed by Russia.

6.2.2 The EU as a normative vs geopolitical actor in the eastern neighbourhood

Given the nature of the dynamics in the common neighbourhood, Makarychev and Devyatkov (2014) argue that the EU itself has been increasingly pushed to become a geostrategic actor in its eastern neighbourhood, in which it is nevertheless significantly limited because of several structural and institutional factors, such as the absence of a military force, that would correspond to the capabilities of Russia.

According to Giusti (2016: 167), the "patchy" response of the EU to the events in Ukraine can be primarily attributed to the limitations that a predominantly normative policy carries with it to the overall development of regional and bilateral relations. Whereas the EU has shaped its relations with the EaP partners chiefly on the normative premise of exporting European values abroad and thereby contributing to the shaping of democratic and peaceful societies, it has failed to take into account the kinds of high politics, the increasingly worsening tensions between the EU and Russia and geopolitical dynamics that played a role in the escalation of the Ukrainian crisis. The focus on the EU's normative discourse has effectively prevented it from an accurate assessment of Russia's interests in the region and the kind of response that the extension of the EU's influence would cause.

Similarly, Sololenko and Hallgren (2015: 4) note that the EU has inevitably become a geopolitical actor in the region even though this has been "without political preparedness". At the same time, geopolitical interests are at the core of Russia's overall policy considerations in the neighbourhood and its evaluation of its partnership with the EU (Zagorski, 2011). To some, the dynamics in the region are essentially characterised by the geopolitical interests of both the EU and Russia. This has at least been at the centre of Russian policy (Ademmer et al., 2016). But as Giusti (2016: 166) notes, the Ukrainian crisis has demonstrated the "EU's inability to foresee and deal with some unintended consequences of its acting as a normative power" notably with regard to the geopolitical dynamics in the region. This is not least due to the fact that although the EU's policies in the region have been based principally on normative considerations, this has been perceived as "little more than a pretext for the pursuit of the national interests of stronger member states" (Sololenko and Hallgren, 2015: 3). There is a clear difference between the perceptions and expectations surrounding the actions of the EU and Russia in the neighbourhood. As Meister (2013) notes, although inside-out the EU's actions in the neighbourhood might be driven by mainly normative considerations, they have hardly ever been perceived as such in Russia.

Some authors also point out the lack of clear definitions of the EU's approach towards Russia and the ambiguity surrounding its policy towards Russia in the common neighbourhood (Sololenko and Hallgren, 2015; Meister, 2013). Sololenko and Hallgren (2015: 1) argue that "the EU has been able to develop effective short-term solutions, but it overlooked some risks and needs to tackle those".

Russia has been accused of taking advantage of the so-called frozen conflicts in the post-Soviet space to maintain influence over certain regions and the political situation on the ground. One of the most prominent cases is the Nagorno-Karabakh conflict. In light of this, Lebduška and Lidl (2014: 3) recommend that the EU increase its efforts on the resolution of the conflict to "ease the grip of Moscow and its security guarantees" in the region.

The contemporary environment in the eastern ENP dimension, characterised by zero-sum dynamics, requires the EU to reconsider its policy architecture. Arguably, some authors see the EU as too entrenched in its normative rhetoric, which precludes it from effectively responding to Russia's policies towards the neighbourhood. The EU is a party to a geopolitical confrontation while its preparedness is questionable. The EU is not a unitary actor with a clear security strategy vis-à-vis the neighbourhood, which severely limits its ability to engage in a geopolitical battle with Russia over the common neighbourhood.

6.2.3 Influence of the EU and Russia on sectoral convergence

Going beyond geopolitical competition between the EU and Russia over the common neighbourhood, scholars (Ademmer et al., 2016, Buzogány, 2016; Delcour, 2016a; Wetzel, 2016; Wolczuk, 2016) address the impact of the two actors on the domestic reforms of the neighbours in a number of sectors, such as trade, natural resources, migration and mobility. The findings indicate that integration with the EU through the DCFTA or with Russia through the EAEU are disconnected from the actual domestic reforms at the sectoral level. Moreover, Russia is sometimes seen as a possible push factor for more integration with the EU and increased compliance with policy change demanded by the EU under conditionality clauses (Ademmer, 2015).

The role of domestic authorities especially in light of the dynamics between the EU and the Russian Federation deserves further attention. Wisniewski (2013: 1) argues that "authorities in the partner countries, frightened of losing power, tend to use [the ENP] as a counterweight to Russian influence instead of as an opportunity to transform". Assessing the kind of impact that the presence of Russia has had on the considerations of domestic actors in the EaP countries therefore leads to conflicted results. Similarly, the pro-Russian vs pro-EU discourse has in many cases demonstratively been used and exploited by political parties and national and local elites in the region (Sololenko and Hallgren, 2015). This manipulation by political elites has accordingly created an increasingly polarising environment and a state of ambiguity and disorientation in the public discourse. According to Slavkova and Shirinyan (2015: 8), balancing domestic politics between the EU and Russia has often been unfavourable for many of the ENP countries that find themselves at the "unrewarding crossroads" of having to choose how to define themselves geopolitically. The new geopolitical, economic and security threats that could arise for many of the countries in a scenario in which they publicly align themselves with one or the other, such as in the case of Ukraine, is seen as an additional burden on countries undergoing very fundamental and painful structural reforms.

The literature has also addressed the impact of the EU on the domestic politics of neighbours. Sasse (2013: 553) argues that the European Union and the premise of increasing integration with the EU has merely provided "a channel for and reinforcement of an ongoing process of regime change" and strengthened "an existing domestic momentum for democratization". The author shows that assumptions about linkages with 'the West' (including the EU) being positively correlated with democratisation are generally overstated and constitute only a moderate factor.

According to Samokhvalov (2015), the presence of the EU and Russia in domestic politics has resulted in several scenarios, beyond traditional perceptions of the dynamic between the EU and Russia as a zero-sum game and implying situations in which domestic authorities have a choice between pro-European or pro-Russian policy directions. The influence of the EU on domestic politics should not be overestimated, as demonstrated in the example of the 'Euromaidan' protests. The protests only grew significantly in numbers after the regime cracked down and the police violently dispersed the protesters. The major wave of protests therefore came not in response to the government's turn on the European Union, but to the violence it used against protesters.

Although the EU is perceived as an influential actor in sectoral convergence in the eastern neighbourhood, there is a variety of external factors that affect the degree to which the EU is successful in promoting convergence with EU-supported or EU-demanded policies (Langbein, 2013). The most prominent of these factors is Russia, often perceived as the region's "alternative hegemon" attempting to limit the convergence with EU policies in the neighbourhood by strengthening trade relations, increasing investment and so forth (Langbein, 2013; Delcour, 2016a).

A special journal issue edited by Ademmer et al. (2016: 9) analyses "whether the simultaneous presence of the EU and Russia in their contested neighbourhood reinforces, neutralizes or undermines efforts to change sectoral institutions, processes or policies". The authors find that although the influence of the two actors is present at the sectoral level, this influence should be counted more as unintended consequences arising from their bilateral relations with the neighbourhood countries. The evidence presented suggests that the triangular relationship between the two actors and the neighbourhood countries ultimately contributes to the change in sectoral policies demanded by the EU as a supportive factor. As the authors suggest, despite popular belief, the most significant factor in considerations of domestic actors is often domestic politics and dynamics rather than external forces and influences. Comparing energy policy change in Georgia and Armenia, Ademmer (2015) argues that interdependence between domestic actors in the common neighbourhood and Russia incentivises adoption of EU-supported policies, when a given country is highly sensitive but not vulnerable to Russian pressure or leverage.

Similarly, examining the role of non-state actors such as international and multinational companies or stakeholders, Langbein (2013) argues that a high degree of economic dependence on Russia has actually fostered convergence with EU-conditioned rules. Using the case of telecommunications and food safety regulations in Ukraine, Langbein (2013) illustrates how both the EU and Russia can apply passive leverage to incentivise sectoral convergence. At the same time, in the case of some of the sectoral changes witnessed in Ukraine, neither active nor passive leverage has supported sectoral convergence with EU rules and policies. Instead, sectoral convergence is rather achieved as a by-product of active leverage exercised by (especially Western) European multinational companies operating in Ukraine.

At the same time, Buzogány (2016) argues that significant political events causing the worsening of relations between neighbourhood countries and the Russian Federation can further strengthen the incentives provided to domestic actors to comply with EU sectoral policies. As demonstrated in the case of Ukraine, the conflict between Kiev and Moscow has allegedly resulted in faster implementation of reforms and harmonisation with EU-supported rules and regulations.

The influence of Russia on sectoral convergence of the EaP states is one of the most contentious issues. While some authors argue that the presence of Russia increases the likelihood and effectiveness of convergence with EU-demanded policies, others view Russia as exercising active leverage that creates unfavourable conditions for the EaP states to internalise EU rules and norms. It is nonetheless clear that macro-level alliances of the EaP states (association agreements/DCFTAs or the Eurasian Economic Union) do not translate into a domestic change and have to be assessed on a case-by-case basis.

6.2.4 Ukraine

Numerous authors have analysed Russia's reaction to the EaP since the re-launch of the Eurasian integration initiative (Zagorski, 2011; Averre, 2011; Kanet and Raquel Freire, 2012; Dragneva and Wolczuk, 2013, 2015; Delcour et al., 2015) and the EU's policies towards the frozen conflicts in the ENP countries (Popescu, 2012; Giumelli, 2011). Still, it has primarily been the crisis in Ukraine that has significantly expanded the academic and policy-oriented literature devoted to the issue of the "common neighbourhood" (Bond, 2014; Delcour and Kostanyan, 2014, Samokhvalov, 2015; Sherr, 2015; Kostanyan and Meister, 2016; Ademmer et al., 2016; Korosteleva, 2016a and 2016b). The case of Ukraine has therefore not only been used to illustrate the EU's policy towards its eastern neighbours, but also its ability and effectiveness to react in times of escalating crisis with both its partners and the Russian Federation as an external yet pivotal actor.

The Ukrainian case remains one of the most intensely studied in the ENP literature. For several authors (Liik, 2014; Kasciunas et al., 2014; Kobzova, 2015), the events in Ukraine constituted a major breaking point in the EU's policy towards the neighbourhood as well as its perception of the role of Russia in the common neighbourhood. Furthermore, at a regional level, the events in Ukraine and the EU's response have considerably affected the way in which both the EU and Russia are perceived (Korosteleva, 2016b). In the case of the EU, numerous questions have been raised among the ENP partners in the east about the EU's commitment, legitimacy and vision for the region, while the Russian regime has enjoyed a surge in confidence domestically (Korosteleva, 2016b).

In 2013, the contestation by Russia of the EU's influence sparked the Euromaidan demonstrations, with Ukrainians protesting the decision of former President Victor Yanukovych not to sign the negotiated association agreement with the EU. Under pressure from increasing civil unrest and public outrage with the decision, Yanukovych fled the country, eventually claiming exile in Russia. Russia reacted to the turn of events in Ukraine by annexing the Crimean Peninsula and actively engaging in hostilities, particularly in the Eastern Ukrainian region of Donbas, attracting criticism not only from European political elites but also from a significant swathe of the international community (Kasciuvas et al., 2014). Since the beginning of hostilities, Russia has been accused of actively supporting the separatist movements in the Donetsk and Luhansk regions, which have to date resulted in several thousand casualties (Kobzova, 2015). By contrast, some authors are critical of the EU (Sakwa, 2016) and others outright blame the West for having caused the crisis in Ukraine (Mearsheimer, 2014).

The treatment of Ukraine demonstrates several characteristics of Russian interests as well as strategies in the neighbourhood. The main consideration for an intervention in Ukraine has been to prevent further integration with the EU, which would have put the future success of the Eurasian Customs Union at stake (Meister, 2013). The instrumentalisation of the separatist movements in eastern Ukraine is also a recurring aspect in the analysis of Russian foreign policy (Kobzova, 2015). In the case of Moldova, "Moscow [has been] actively using separatist forces in Gagauzia and Transnistria to put further pressure on Chisinau" (Kobzova, 2015: 3).

Delcour and Kostanyan (2014: 1) argue that the conflict in Ukraine has exacerbated the divisions between the neighbourhood countries while effectively forcing them to choose between a path to European integration on the one hand, or Eurasian integration under Russian leadership on the other, resulting in a 'lose–lose' situation. The case of Ukraine also highlights the gap in public opinion caused by EU–Russia rivalry. As Rieker (2014) shows, partnership with either the EU or Russia is supported by similar shares of the population. However, opinion polls show the marked differentiation between the young and older generations, with the younger ones significantly favouring integration with the EU.

The crisis in Ukraine has resulted in numerous debates contemplating the future of EU–Russia relations, as well as the future of both actors' policies in the neighbourhood (Kasciunas et al., 2014; Hett et al., 2014, Trenin, 2016). The question remains of whether the zero-sum dynamics can be overcome, or whether the 'common neighbourhood' will continue to represent a major area of contestation between Brussels and Moscow. Techau (2014) states that Russia will never accept the existing security and political architecture in the wider European space, will not concede to an expansionary EU, and will not accept a scenario in which European states have the same say as Russia in determining the political future of the neighbourhood. At the same time, the literature also describes other scenarios concerning the future development of EU–Russia relations, including one of prevailing realism and pragmatism, the emergence of a new partnership between the EU and Russia based on common interests and the de-politicisation of energy. An increasingly unstable neighbourhood characterised by EU–Russia competition is also a plausible scenario (Hett et al., 2014).

In sum, while some authors argue for strengthening the cooperation with Russia to avoid an EU–Russia conflict in the future, others highlight the effects of the Ukrainian crisis on the EU's policies towards the EaP countries. Ukraine demonstrates not only the highly contested nature of the geopolitical environment but also the need for the EU to show strong commitment to its neighbourhood at a time when a more assertive Russia is challenging the EU's policies vis-à-vis the region.

6.3 Conclusion

To conclude, there is more literature addressing external actors vis-à-vis the eastern neighbourhood than the southern dimension of the ENP. The 2008 war in Georgia and the recent political events in Ukraine have brought the role of Russia in the eastern neighbourhood into the spotlight of ENP research. A large number of sources concentrate on the dynamic between the EU and Russia and the impact of this dynamic on domestic developments as well as the domestic policy preferences of the countries in the common neighbourhood.

The literature on the southern neighbourhood is focused on the relationship between the ENP and the EU's wider regional policy frameworks and the role of the neighbours of the neighbours. Nevertheless, in light of the rapidly changing regional dynamics and the current security challenges following the Arab revolutions, there is need for an in-depth analysis of the extent and nature of the involvement of external actors in the southern Mediterranean and the MENA region.

The impact of involvement by global actors such as China and the US in the EU's southern neighbourhood is likewise under-researched. Also less clear are the ways in which the rapidly changing, post-Arab Spring geopolitical environment in the Middle East and the war in Syria are affecting the role of external actors, such as Iran and the Gulf states, in the southern neighbourhood. Indeed, there is a fundamental lack of scholarship directly addressing the influence of regional or global actors on the ENP in the southern neighbourhood.

Furthermore, factors such as climate change, migratory pressures and radicalisation, which are expected to be influential in the current socio-economic and political landscapes in the individual ENP countries and which are often quoted as such, are nevertheless absent from more focused analysis directly relating to the ENP.

As mentioned in previous chapters, external and regional actors can also demonstratively influence the perception of European values or the European Union in general. While supporting their own representation of value systems, such actors can potentially undermine the visibility and credibility of the EU, which to a large extent portrays itself as a normative actor. The literature points to the necessity of assessing the influence of external actors also on the normative considerations of national and local elites.

There is a rapidly increasing body of the literature concerning the role of Russia in the EaP states. However, some elements remain ambiguous. First, it is unclear to what extent the Russian presence in the region has had an impact on domestic policy preferences and sectoral convergence. While some authors suggest that political and economic pressure from the Kremlin has in several instances precluded countries in the eastern neighbourhood from pursuing deeper integration with the EU, others suggest that political and economic interdependencies with Russia have constituted a positive factor in convergence with EU policies. Second, disagreements exist as to what constitutes the basis for the current nature of Russian foreign policy and engagement in the region. Some argue that Russia has actively developed an assertive foreign policy based on its strategic considerations, but others see this development merely as a response to the expansion of the EU's presence in the region.

7. COHERENCE

Analysing the concept of coherence, Gebhard (2011) notes that "despite its over-use in the literature and in political debate, the notion of coherence is among the most frequently misinterpreted and misused concepts in EU foreign policy". Therefore, this literature overview conceptualises coherence in the ENP at three interrelated levels. At the horizontal level, the principle concerns the coherence between the EU's external (and internal) policies, the policy objectives (i.e. short-term security and stability, and long-term respect for values and prosperity) and instruments. Vertical coherence pertains to the need for EU and member state policies to complement and strengthen each other (Hertog and Stross, 2013). Institutional coherence covers inter- and intra-institutional dimensions in order to overcome 'turf wars' within and between the Council, the Commission and the EEAS.

7.1 Horizontal coherence

The literature discusses the lack of coherence in and between the different ENP policy objectives, instruments and methodologies. Different ENP instruments do not mutually reinforce the various ENP policy objectives. For example, Koenig (2013) observes a lack of horizontal coherence at the intersection of the Union's human rights and humanitarian policies and the measures used for migration management. Specifically, in the past, Frontex had repeatedly been blamed for failing to rescue migrants at sea and to meet international human rights standards. But the hands of Frontex are tied by the limited assets at this agency's disposal. In fact, the Italian authorities themselves have provided all the naval assets and staff for operation Hermes. Furthermore, Frontex neither has a protection mandate nor particular human rights expertise.

Thus, the added value of Frontex is very limited in view of the EU's humanitarian aid and human rights objectives.

In the Mediterranean context the role of the EUSR to promote coherence in the EU's policies and instruments in the region has been criticised. The mandate of the EU special representative made particular reference to ensuring "coherence, consistency and coordination of the Union and Member States' policies and actions towards the region". Several task forces led by the EUSR for the southern Mediterranean have been used to secure the coordination of the EU's action and to bring together the assorted political bodies and economic institutions to streamline the EU's support for the Arab transitions. Morillas (2015) illustrates that the EUSR's success in promoting coherence between the EU instruments and policies depends on the stability of the domestic authorities in the ENP countries and how they perceive the EU. For example, in Tunisia the task force was rather successful in the coordination of various public and private bodies with a specific emphasis on economic cooperation, trade, market access and reform of the rule of law and the judiciary, among other aspects. This was mainly because the EU and Tunisia had strong relations (in terms of trade relations as well as economic and financial assistance after the revolution), which favoured the recognition of the EU as a powerful external actor and its leverage in providing support for the transition. In Libya, however, the task force aimed to strengthen the coherence of crisis management activities, the interaction between the different actors involved in the crisis response, the coordination with EU member states' bilateral policies and with other international organisations. Yet in this case, the lack of a central authority and a governance system in the country have impeded streamlining the coordination of EU activities through a task force similar to the one in Tunisia.

As illustrated further on in this study, there is a consensus in the literature about a lack of horizontal coherence between two key ENP objectives. When facing an interests-vs-values dilemma, the EU prioritises the former in the context of the ENP (see chapter 3). Still, it also needs to be noted in this context that there is a lack of coherence among the different values the EU aims to export. Gstöhl (2016b) notes that especially economic and political values can be at odds. The Union faces the general problem of how to prioritise among the disparate values the ENP wants to export. Art. 21 TEU does not provide a ranking of objectives. Conflicts may also arise within the same group of values, for instance between sustainable development and poverty reduction on the one hand (e.g. as enshrined in the DCFTAs with Ukraine, Moldova and Georgia) and trade liberalisation on the other.

Gstöhl (2015) argues that there should be coherence between the geographical policy frameworks, i.e. between the ENP and the EU's policies towards the neighbours of the neighbours. For example, ENP instruments could be applied to the neighbours of the neighbours and these countries should be involved in different ENP programmes, instruments and strategies. This can happen in sectoral cooperation (e.g. strengthening and broadening the INOGATE programme or the TRACECA programme) or by connecting them through trade and infrastructure networks (e.g. expanding the energy community or European common aviation area to the broader neighbourhood).

Several aspects of ENP instruments have been regarded as beneficial for the promotion of coherence throughout the policy framework. Although the ENP action plans were criticised for including too many vague and conflicting objectives (cf. *infra*) and because they were not legally binding on their authors, it has also been argued that their soft-law nature made a coherent approach in the ENP possible since they could be adopted swiftly, without inter-institutional competence battles (Van der Loo, 2016a; Van Vooren, 2012). This was particularly important for the action plans and association agendas because they have a 'cross-pillar' dimension, covering issues ranging from trade and economic cooperation to political dialogue, human rights and fundamental freedoms.

At the horizontal level, the EU has demonstrated significant incoherence among the different ENP objectives. Democracy, human rights and support of civil society continue to constitute the main priorities on paper but security and stability are prioritised in reality. By analysing the assorted ENP action plans, Börzel and Van Hüllen (2014) argue that the EU "sends one message with one voice but pursues conflicting goals". They hold that the EU is characterised by substantive inconsistency rather than a lack of internal cohesiveness. They illustrate that this 'democratisation-stabilisation dilemma' becomes more pronounced the less democratic and stable the regimes to which the EU is sending its message. For example, although the action plans with the ENP countries pay tribute to democracy, human rights and the rule of law, they lean more towards state building than democratic change. There is the risk that the goal of promoting democracy will conflict with that of promoting effective governance, because democratic change entails the risk of destabilisation: it requires a transition of power and regime change, which can lead to political uncertainty about the outcome of the process. As Börzel and Van Hüllen argue, "promoting democracy is likely to thwart stability in the short run". The authors even come to the conclusion that the more precarious the situation in a non-democratic country is, the more likely the EU will seek to stabilise the existing regime, at the cost of the democratisation objective. Several other authors come to the same conclusion on the basis of empirical research. Dandashly (2015) illustrates that the EU has not moved away from its previous prioritisation of security over democracy promotion. Although democracy promotion as a goal became a priority with the outbreak of the Arab Spring, with the deterioration of stability in the southern neighbourhood, security and stability have once again emerged as the EU's primary concerns. The EU's policy towards Tunisia, Egypt and Libya demonstrates that political and socio-economic instability have pushed the EU to invest in the security of the region, at the expense of democracy promotion. Irregular migration, the rise of extremism and Islamic fundamentalism as well as the increasing number of terrorist threats remain issues of short-term concern (Dandashly, 2015).

Börzel and Lebanidze (2015) also argue that political conditionality has been used inconsistently, i.e. to different degrees in various cases, leading to a preponderance of a state-building approach rather than democracy promotion. The EU intended to strengthen neighbouring states' capacities in order for them to implement the EU's values and rules. Yet, despite strengthened efforts in the area of state-building, no significant achievements have been recorded in this regard. Some researchers (Wetzel and Orbie, 2012) even argue that this approach might have strengthened autocratic leadership by improving the functions of the bureaucratic apparatus (courts, for example) without delivering on their independence.

In addition, the coherence between the ENP's sectoral cooperation objectives and democracy promotion has been analysed. Freyburg et al. (2011) examine whether and under what conditions sectoral cooperation (e.g. in the areas of competition, environmental and migration policy) promotes democratic governance. They conclude that the promotion of democratic governance through sectoral cooperation is successful when the relevant sectoral *acquis* is concretely specified and detailed and when the cooperation between the EU and ENP states is institutionalised. Lower adoption costs for the implementation of sectoral cooperation are crucial for the promotion of democratic governance. The authors find similar patterns of rule adoption and rule application in Jordan, Morocco, Moldova and Ukraine. However, in both the east and the south, they detect a clear discrepancy between rule adoption and rule application. "Whereas the EU has been fairly successful in inducing the four selected ENP countries to adopt legislation in line with democratic governance provisions, these provisions have – at least so far – generally not been implemented."

In sum, the literature is overwhelmingly critical of the horizontal incoherence of the EU's policy vis-à-vis the neighbourhood as it appears that the different ENP objectives and instruments do not mutually reinforce each other. Numerous authors claim that the ENP lacks a clear set of objectives, making the ENP a fuzzy undertaking, and they argue that the EU should prioritise and have clearly defined objectives.

7.2 Vertical coherence

Vertical coherence refers to the convergence of strategic interests, goals, policy initiatives, financial assistance and technical support between the EU and the member states' bilateral relations with the neighbourhood countries. Bringing about coherence between the member states and the EU has been especially challenging. There is little literature on vertical coherence, namely, the extent to which member states' and EU policies are aligned. This section mainly focuses on divergent positions between member states (Section 3.2 of this report touched upon the issue of the vertical coherence).

In terms of policy formulation and implementation, the EU has often been able to act only at the level of the lowest common denominator due to the divergent positions of individual member states (Kostanyan and Orbie, 2013; Comelli, 2013). Because of national considerations and the interests of the member states, "the ENP has [so far] been successful in technical cooperation; however, in order to also achieve their political goals, member states must reconsider their tendency to protect their national interests, often at the expense of common objectives" (Maurer and Simao, 2013: 14).

As mentioned in previous chapters, the lack of vertical coherence and its negative impact on the EU's effectiveness has been proven in several studies. Parkes and Sobják (2014) illustrate that the lack of a coherent approach among the member states towards Russia affects the EU's ability to speak with one voice. Koenig (2013) demonstrates the lack of vertical consistency during the first phase of the Libyan crisis, when France immediately recognised the Transitional National Council (TNC) as the sole legitimate representative of the Libyan people. This unilateral move displeased the other member states, which argued that it prevented the evaluation of a common EU strategy towards the TNC. Another example was the German position with regard to the military operation in Libya, as Germany broke ranks with its EU and NATO partners when it abstained in the vote on UN Security Council Resolution 1973.

The lack of vertical coherence is also visible in the EU's sanction policy towards Russia. The EU agreed rather swiftly to impose a set of sanctions on Russia in June and July 2014 "in response to Russia's actions in the east of Ukraine". On 19 March 2015, the European Council agreed to link the duration of the sanctions to the complete implementation of the Minsk agreements and in July 2016, after having assessed the implementation of the Minsk agreements, the Council decided to renew the sanctions for a further six months, until 31 January 2017. Although the Minsk agreements are far from being implemented, the consensus in the EU to extend the sanctions has become increasingly shaky. Dolidze (2015) argues that especially the member states that depend on Russia in different economic fields "are trying to take the middle-way position between Brussels and Kremlin", and Kostanyan and Meister (2016) illustrate that in particular, Italy, Greece, Cyprus,

Austria and Hungary, and some politicians in Germany and France, have come out against extending sanctions. According to Kostanyan and Meister, the EU's inability to prolong sanctions will "send the message to Moscow, that the destabilisation of countries in the common neighbourhood, including via military action, will have very limited or no consequences". Even if the sanctions are limited, Kostanyan and Meister claim that they are an important instrument to show unity and to draw a red line demarcating unacceptable Russian action. The lack of a unified position on the extension of sanctions would be a missed opportunity because they argue that in the context of the global economic slowdown, together with low energy prices and bad economic policy in Moscow, these economic sanctions do affect the Russian economy, and thus increase the bargaining power of the EU. However, Wesslau (2016) is more positive and believes that the member states will remain united on this issue as long as the Minsk agreements are not fully implemented. He believes that "EU member states recognise that Russia is a divisive issue and that the existing unity has been hard-won and is fragile" and to break that unity would amount to vetoing a set policy that a large constituency of member states feels strongly about. At the same time, Wesslau (2016) warns that sanctions could be taken hostage by a member state to gain concessions in other areas. For example, in December 2015 Italy's former Prime Minister Matteo Renzi blocked a technical rollover of the sanctions and demanded a political discussion. His move did not have much to do with the merits of sanctions, but rather his irritation with Berlin over Nordstream II and his efforts to relax EU rules on budgets.

The member states' diverse positions also became visible during the negotiations of the association agreements with the EaP countries, especially with regard to a membership prospect in those agreements. During the negotiations on the EU–Moldova Association Agreement, around ten member states (including Romania, Poland, the Baltic States and the Czech Republic) were ready to upgrade their relationship with Moldova and would have agreed to move the country from the ENP to the enlargement sphere. A smaller group of three to five member states (including France, Italy and Spain) clearly opposed the idea. The rest of the member states acted as fence-sitters and could be swayed one way or the other (Kostanyan, 2014a). The same positions were also taken by the same member states during the negotiations on the EU–Ukraine Association Agreement. The lack of a unified and firm EU position provided the Ukrainian negotiators with the opportunity to use the membership card to gain concessions in other areas of the negotiations, though without much success (Van der Loo, 2016a). The final compromise was that the association agreements only recognise the European ambitions of the partner countries (without a specific membership commitment), but do not explicitly preclude accession in the long term.

Comelli (2013) argues that the merit of the ENP with regard to vertical coherence is that it creates a single framework for all relations between all the EU member states with all the neighbouring countries. Therefore, the eastern member states have to deal with the Mediterranean countries and the southern member states have to deal with the EaP countries. The flip side is that the ENP "has often come to represent only the minimum common denominator among the different positions taken by Member States" (Comelli, 2013: 3). Moreover, this author argues that the ENP is mainly dealt with in a technocratic way by the Commission and the EEAS, whereas the member states have their own policies and can count on many other resources, leading to a 're-nationalisation' of the ENP. But not everybody agrees that a single framework for all neighbouring countries is positive. Witney and Dworkin (2012) conclude that "the unhappy way in which Brussels puts all 'neighbourhood' funding into one pot (...) creates a zero-sum game between southern and eastern neighbourhoods [and] inevitably splits the member states into the natural east-prioritising and south-prioritising camps".

Vertical coherence can only be improved if member states are willing to work together and coordinate their national foreign policies. If they choose to ignore this concept of 'mutual accountability' developed by EU actors, and reject the idea of adapting their national policies to EU approaches, it is likely that the level of vertical coherence will remain unchanged. (Maurer and Simao, 2013). Yet, as mentioned previously, there is a significant level of disagreement between the individual member states as to what constitutes European 'interests' in the neighbourhood and what represents the common European values that the EU seeks to export through the ENP.

To conclude, there is a strong consensus in the literature that vertical coherence in the ENP is weak. The member states have disparate policy interests and take actions that preclude a coherent EU approach towards the neighbouring countries. At the same time, the literature provides empirical evidence of vertical incoherence in CFSP-related cases (e.g. sanctions of military operations), although this is not sufficiently demonstrated in the sectoral areas of the ENP. Ultimately, in order to have a better understanding of the vertical coherence in the ENP, more research needs to be carried out on the alignment of the EU member state policies with that of the EU vis-à-vis the neighbourhood.

7.3   Intra- and inter-institutional coherence

The literature also examines the intra- and inter-institutional incoherence within the framework of the ENP. The establishment of the EEAS and the reconfigured post of the High Representative for Foreign Affairs and Security Policy/Vice-President of the Commission (HR/VP) aimed at bringing about more coherence to the EU's external action in general and the ENP in particular (Blockmans and Hillion, 2013a and 2013b). Although the collaboration between the EEAS and the Commission in the area of the ENP is highly complex, there is a consensus in the literature that it has proven to work rather well. When the EEAS was established in 2011, most Commission staff members working on the ENP were transferred to the new Service. The Commissioner for Enlargement and his cabinet were the only Commission officials that still dealt specifically with the ENP. Having a commissioner responsible for the European Neighbourhood Policy but without a DG has defined the first years of EEAS relations with the Commission. Thanks to a division of labour with the previous HR/VP, Catherine Ashton, the EEAS divisions dealing with the ENP became the de facto service of Commissioner Stefan Füle. The EEAS units working on the ENP collaborated well with Commissioner Füle, who became an ally of the EEAS inside the Commission (Helwig et al., 2013). The EU's initial reaction to the Arab Spring and the 2011 ENP Review are considered good examples of coherence coordination between these two institutions because the EEAS was able "to put on the table the full toolbox of Union measures" (Wouters et al., 2013: 54). For example, in the course of the Arab Spring, the Commission developed the Communication on "Partnership for Democracy and Shared Prosperity" in close coordination with the EEAS. At the top level, the Commissioner responsible for the ENP and the HR/VP coordinated their policies by organising meetings between the respective cabinets and the sharing of documents. This positive performance is partially attributed to the fact that both the EEAS and the Commission prioritised the ENP (Wouters et al., 2013: 55).

Although the EEAS swiftly took up its role in the ENP, it is closely monitored by the member states. Kostanyan and Orbie (2013) illustrate that the discretionary power of the EEAS in the EaP's multilateral track is limited because its activities are strictly monitored and controlled by the member states in multiple fora, such as the COEST working party in the Council, the Political and Security Committee, the COREPER and the Foreign Affairs Council. Moreover, they illustrate that also the European Commission, the European Parliament and the Eastern Partnership Civil Society Forum further limit the discretionary power of the EEAS in the EaP's multilateral track, so that its power cannot exceed that of the highest common denominator between a wide range of stakeholders (cf. *supra*).

In the area of the ENP the EEAS also has to collaborate on a continual basis with a number of Commission DGs, including those for Energy (ENER), Home Affairs (HOME), and International Cooperation and Development (DEVCO). It is considered that the coordination between the EEAS and these Commission DGs has functioned well but could be improved (Maurer and Simao, 2013). Divergences between the EEAS and various Commission DGs emerged especially during the implementation of the ENP Communications. For example, the EEAS seeks general visa liberalisation for the ENP countries, while DG HOME takes a stance closer to the member states' interior ministries, which are rather sceptical towards the further opening of borders to immigrants (Sek, 2013). Also the cooperation between the EEAS and the Commission with regard to the EU's humanitarian aid response to the Libyan crisis was problematic. Whereas humanitarian aid is supposed to be coordinated by the EEAS department for crisis response, the coordination with DG ECHO was insufficient due to bureaucratic competition and turf battles (Koenig, 2013). In the area of energy, the March 2011 ENP Communication spelled out the ambition to invite southern ENP countries to join the Energy Community Treaty. However, this was clearly a foreign policy objective pursued by the EEAS that was not supported by DG ENER (Wouters et al., 2013). Conversely, EEAS working relations with the member states are considered efficient. In some cases, when the problem exceeds the boundaries of its discretionary power, the EEAS goes back to the member states (Kostanyan, 2013).

The literature also explores institutional coherence with regard to the EU's representation in the neighbourhood, as the President of the European Council and the HR/VP continue to represent the EU in addition to the President of the Commission and the Commissioner for Enlargement and the ENP. A practice has developed in relation to political démarches addressed to the neighbouring states, where the Commissioner for Enlargement and ENP and the HR/VP (acting on behalf of the member states) jointly issue statements regarding political developments in the neighbourhood. While this creates a united front, it is nevertheless problematic as it sometimes leads to a slower and softer reaction on behalf of the EU given the necessity of reaching a common understanding among all the actors involved (Ghazaryan, 2014). Moreover, it is also noted that the need to speak with one voice should not be exaggerated. For example, the first EU reactions to the Libyan crisis were declarations from the HR/VP on behalf of the EU, followed by similar statements by the Presidents of the European Council, European Parliament and the European Commission. Since these statements were initially consistent with one another as well with other EU documents (Natorski, 2016), the result was a "constructive polyphony", which added "strength and coverage to the message at hand" (Koenig, 2013: 8). Still, in a second stage HR/VP Ashton and President of the European Council Herman Van Rompuy issued increasingly divergent statements on the goal of military intervention in Libya, which resulted in a cacophony.

The coordination among the EU institutions during the negotiations on the association agreements and DCFTAs has also been analysed. While the EEAS is in charge of negotiations on political association and security cooperation, DG Trade was responsible for the DCFTA negotiations. Moreover, in the areas of sectoral cooperation pertinent to the association agreements, the EEAS has had to rely extensively on the expertise of different European Commission DGs (e.g. on energy, transport and financial services). In the case of the negotiations on the EU–Moldova Association Agreement, the EEAS aimed to negotiate as ambitious and forward-looking an agreement as possible. The control exercised by the member states and the checks applied by the Commission considerably limited the discretion of the EEAS in pursuing the agreement and the DCFTA between the EU and Moldova (Kostanyan, 2014a). For example, EEAS discretion was initially constrained by DG Trade on the issue of the start of DCFTA talks. Unlike the EEAS, which considered Moldova politically important, DG Trade viewed Moldova as 'insignificant' in terms of trade. Initially, DG Trade was therefore not eager to devote its limited resources to EU–Moldova trade negotiations. The discretion of the EEAS was also further limited by the member states' detailed negotiation mandate, especially in those areas that are sensitive to them (e.g. political dialogue, foreign and security policy, and freedom, security and justice). Overall, however, the member states were rather positive towards the work of the EEAS, "both in terms of the latter's respect for the red lines outlined by the member states and regarding the good and rapid progress of the negotiations" (Kostanyan, 2014a: 391). With regard to the DCFTA negotiations, DG Trade was assisted on several chapters by other relevant DGs (e.g. for competition, intellectual property rights and energy). Concerning the EU–Ukraine Association Agreement, the lack of a consistent language on legislative approximation in the text of the DCFTA was attributed to the fact that each DG used a different legal term for defining the specific legislative approximation commitments. During the 'legal scrubbing phase' of the agreement, this inconsistency was not noted by the lawyer linguist, leading to an inconsistent "patchwork" of legislative approximation clauses in the DCFTA, which will further complicate the implementation of these complex trade agreements (Van der Loo, 2016a).

The role of EU agencies in the ENP is hardly analysed in the literature. Although the Commission stressed the importance of opening up EU agencies to ENP countries, participation has remained largely a theoretical possibility (Chamon, 2016). In the area of mobility and border management, however, the role of

Frontex with respect to the ENP countries has been criticised because the lack of transparency and accountability of the working arrangements that Frontex has concluded with several Mediterranean ENP countries can negatively affect the fundamental rights of migrants (Bonavita, 2015).

Finally, the impact of the new 'neighbourhood clause', introduced by the Lisbon Treaty (Art. 8 TEU), on the ENP's coherence is explored. This provision states that "the Union shall develop a special relationship with neighbouring countries, aiming to establish an area of prosperity and good neighbourliness, founded on the values of the Union and characterised by close and peaceful relations based on cooperation". Hillion (2014) argues that Art. 8 TEU may contribute to the cohesion of the ENP because it is positioned outside the chapter on the CFSP in the TEU, meaning that it should not be affected by the pillar politics deriving from the recurrent distinction between CFSP and non-CFSP powers of the Union. It also consolidates the comprehensive character of the ENP. Moreover, its location outside the provisions on 'EU external action' suggests, according to Hillion, that the ENP is conceived as a policy with both internal and external dimensions, so that EU institutions have to take into account the ENP goals when exercising their EU competences, for instance in elaborating the EU's transport, energy and environment policies. Art. 8 also encapsulates a normative shift in the EU's policy towards its neighbours as the article refers to the promotion of "the values of the Union", and not the shared values or common values referred to in previous ENP documents (Van Elsuwege and Petrov 2011; Hillion, 2014). This makes the ENP objectives more coherent with the general obligations of the EU to uphold its values in the world (Art. 3(5) TEU). Yet in practice the impact of the catch-all Art. 8 is limited, especially when considering that it was hardly mentioned in the latest two reviews of the ENP.

7.4 Is coherence a precondition for effectiveness?

A majority of scholars argue that coherence is a factor contributing to the effectiveness or credibility of the EU (Schumacher, 2012; Balfour, 2012a). Börzel and Van Hüllen (2014) conclude that the inherent tensions between ENP objectives (democratisation and stabilisation) hamper the effectiveness of the ENP to promote democratic change through the EU's neighbourhood reform agenda. Wouters et al. (2013) present a more nuanced picture, arguing that coherence and coordination between the EEAS and the Commission has been positive especially during the Arab Spring and the 2011 Review of the ENP. The assessment is nonetheless negative when it comes to effective implementation of the policies on the ground.

While several authors acknowledge that coherence can be beneficial for an effective ENP policy, they also argue that coherence should not be equated with effectiveness (Thomas, 2012). Van Vooren maintains that even if a policy is coherent with EU fundamental values, there is no guarantee that the EU's approach actually prompts the desired effect on the ground (2012: 287). Natorski (2016) is even more critical, as he claims that the Lisbon Treaty's institutional architecture formalises this coherence objective and considerably limits the room for policy innovation in the ENP. "As a result, pre-existing policy has persisted because actors involved in the debate on policy change irreflexively limited their scope for alternatives by thinking in terms of coherence" (Natorksi, 2016: 663). The author illustrates that the appeal to coherence explains why the 2011 ENP Review did not radically change the basic assumptions, objectives and instruments of the ENP. He also argues that this coherence limited the EU's policy space during the Arab Spring. For example, the search for coherence between the EU's military presence and humanitarian engagement in Libya initially blocked a CSDP action in the southern Mediterranean.

7.5 Conclusion

After the entry into force of the Lisbon Treaty numerous studies explored the impact of the institutional reforms (e.g. the establishment of the EEAS and the position of the HR/VP) on the coherence of the EU's external action. Still, the amount of literature that explicitly analyses coherence in the ENP is rather limited. Moreover, coherence is a fuzzy and often misinterpreted concept in EU external relations and only a few authors try to operationalise this concept or aim to bridge the political science and legal debate on this ambiguous term. There is no consistent approach towards the conceptualisation of coherence in the study of the EU's external relations, which complicates the formulation of general conclusions about the EU's coherence in the ENP. Nevertheless, several observations can be drawn from the literature on this topic.

First, the literature is overwhelmingly critical about horizontal coherence in the ENP. The different ENP instruments are perceived not to mutually reinforce the various ENP policy objectives. The EU's ability to promote coherence among its instruments depends on the domestic situations in the ENP countries. The more stable, democratic and 'EU-friendly' the ENP country is, the more coherent can be the deployment of the EU's instruments. There is also a broad consensus that there is an incoherence among the diverse ENP objectives. Notably, it appears that the EU has preferred its 'stabilisation' objective to the 'democratisation' objective. Most, but not all, studies on this point are based on empirical research, mainly analysing the different EU instruments (e.g. the action plans) and actors. Unfortunately, when relying on case studies, only a few studies select ENP countries from both the east and the south. Therefore, it is difficult to generalise the research findings for the entire ENP. For example, whereas there is a consensus in the literature that in the EU's policy response to the Arab Spring the stabilisation objective was – and still is – pursued at the cost of the democratisation objective, there is no strong empirical evidence that this also applies for the eastern ENP countries.

Additionally, there is consensus in the literature that the degree of vertical coherence is insufficient. EU member states in particular were not capable of 'speaking with one voice' in the context of the Arab Spring. Whereas it is recognised that the EU member states swiftly agreed to adopt sanctions against Russia for its role in the Ukraine crisis, several authors doubt whether the member states will be able to extend the sanctions in the future, even if the Minsk agreements are not entirely implemented. It is argued that due to the divergent positions of individual member states, the EU is only able to act at the level of the lowest common denominator. However, where empirical research illustrates that this is indeed largely true for the 'hard security' or CFSP-related cases, this 're-nationalisation' of the ENP cannot be detected in the more sectoral or technocratic instruments and policies of the ENP.

In the latter cases, the leading role of the Commission and the EEAS avoid vertical incoherence.

The majority of authors are more positive with regard to the EU's intra- and inter-institutional coherence. Although the collaboration between the EEAS and the Commission in the area of the ENP is highly complex, there is a consensus in the literature, based on solid empirical research (i.e. mainly interviews with officials of the different EU institutions), that it has proven to work rather well. Yet the coordination between the EEAS and different Commission DGs could be improved. The discretionary power of the EEAS is limited in the ENP, as illustrated during the negotiations on the association agreements, because its activities are closely monitored and controlled by the member states.

Most authors also claim that coherence is a precondition for an effective ENP, although these claims are not based on empirical research. Nevertheless, it seems obvious that coherence is beneficial for the effectiveness of the ENP. If the EU institutions, member states, instruments and policy objectives are mutually reinforcing in the context of the ENP, it is very likely that the EU's interventions (output) will contribute more to the achievement of the policy objectives (outcome). This effect should not be exaggerated, however, because even if the EU's ENP instruments and objectives are coherent, there is no guarantee that the EU's approach will produce the desired effect. In sum, coherence contributes to the effectiveness of the ENP, but it is not a sufficient condition for its effectiveness.

8. LOOKING BACK TO LOOK AHEAD: THE 2015 ENP REVIEW

Less than four years after the first ENP Review was conducted in 2011, the EU launched another one by issuing a Joint Consultation Paper on 4 March 2015, promising a thorough re-examination of its neighbourhood policy. This latest ENP Review, which is based on contributions from 250 stakeholders in the EU and the ENP countries, stresses stabilisation, differentiation and ownership and is more grounded in the realities of the region. In this concluding section, the report analyses the 2015 ENP Review through the prism of the literature review, paying particular attention to the factors informing the ENP's effectiveness and coherence.

The 2015 Review has significant implications for the conditionality in the EU's relations with the ENP countries. By stressing differentiation, the ENP Review breaks from the EU's traditional 'take-it-or-leave-it' approach. For example, prior to the 2015 Review, the EU offered the neighbouring countries association agreements and DCFTAs. They had to either accept or reject entering into extended negotiations on these rather in-depth agreements. The Review has changed this approach and the first serious attempt to apply differentiation in a contractual sense is the EU's negotiation of a new framework agreement with Armenia (Kostanyan and Giragosian, 2016). With the new agreement, the EU aspires to pave a third way, i.e. a less deep and comprehensive agreement, which, among other things, takes into account Armenia's commitments under the Eurasian Economic Union.

Although a majority of the authors reviewed in this report had argued in favour of a differentiated approach long before the 2015 ENP Review, some scholars identified a number of limitations and risks inherent to the approach. First, excessive differentiation might undermine the ENP as a common framework and it does not offer anything new to the neighbours that have already concluded an association agreement and DCFTA with the EU (Kostanyan, 2016b). The new ENP promises ever-greater differentiation without translating the concept into practical terms (Delcour, 2015b) and clarifying what it means beyond allowing the neighbours to cherry-pick the policies they wish to take part in (Schumacher, 2016a).

More fundamentally, differentiation risks weakening the EU's normative agenda and might further undermine the effectiveness of the conditionality. In fact, the Review abandons the idealistic goals of the ENP and the Treaty of Lisbon and "represents little more than an elegantly crafted fig leaf that purports to be a strategic approach to the EU's outer periphery, but masks an inclination towards a more hard-nosed Realpolitik", which is akin to more standard EU foreign policy (Blockmans, 2015: 1). Some scholars even state that as far as the southern neighbourhood is concerned, the new ENP is a defeat of reformists who expected a normative and value-based policy from the EU (Schumacher, 2016a: 1). The text of the Joint Communication on the 2015 Review, as well as the statements by the High Representative and the Neighbourhood Commissioner, demonstrate that respect for human rights and democracy are not central elements of the new ENP. There is a valid concern that based on differentiation some neighbours are likely to resist including the human rights agenda in cooperation with the EU, while insisting on policy areas such as security, energy, development and trade (Kostanyan, 2016b).

The 2015 ENP Review is more pragmatic compared with its predecessors (2004 and 2011) when it comes to resolving the interests-vs-values dilemma. As a response to the various ongoing crises in the neighbourhood, the EU has moved away from the ambitious idea of achieving 'deep democracy' and focused on extinguishing the 'ring of fire' that surrounds its borders.

The 2015 Review scales back the ambition of the ENP through incorporating stabilisation as a short- to mid-term goal for the neighbourhood, which complements the original goals of the ENP to achieve stability, security and prosperity. Stabilisation should not be confused with stability, which bears negative connotations due to its association with preserving power in the hands of authoritarian rulers in the ENP states. Instead, it entails helping ENP states and societies to build resilience through providing assistance in conflict resolution and administrative spheres, along with economic and social development according to the articulated needs of recipients (Dworkin and Wesslau, 2015: 10). The assumption is that in working with the neighbouring states, the EU should first aim to achieve the basic political and economic stability that is necessary for ensuring democracy and human rights. Yet, the much-stressed concept of stabilisation only amplifies the concern about the EU's commitment to human rights and democracy.

Acknowledgement of the fact that social and economic inequality is a primary source of instability in the neighbourhood, and that it has to be addressed by the EU, is one of the more constructive points of the reviewed ENP (Biscop, 2016). However, the ENP Review uses the notion of resilience while not clarifying whose and against what this resilience should be achieved, which engenders scepticism regarding the EU's intentions (Koenig, 2016). Therefore, some argue that the EU seeks to create a buffer zone comprised of neighbouring states that would be able to protect the EU from the negative influence of third actors (Biscop, 2016: 17).

Moreover, the vagueness of the terms 'stabilisation' and 'resilience' as well as the absence of any clear indication about how the EU will balance its interests and values in its relations with its neighbours, leaves space for the latter to arbitrarily define the scope of the EU's activities on values promotion (Delcour, 2015b; Schumacher, 2016a). And as the new ENP foresees much more involvement on the part of the EU member states, their individual interests are likely to trump the promotion of the EU's values in the neighbourhood.

When analysing the new ENP through the prism of perceptions, the ENP is no longer recognised as a primarily transformative instrument but rather as a preventive tool used to minimise negative spillovers of the various ongoing crises in the neighbourhood. Hence, the main interest of the EU is to stabilise and strengthen the resilience of its neighbours.

To make the ENP more effective, the EU rightly emphasises the need for more active involvement of its members in the process of policy formation and implementation. Some EU capitals felt disengaged from the ENP while many of the national governments were deliberately limiting their participation in the ENP given their preference for bilateral cooperation with partners. Thus, the ownership principle emphasised in the ENP is supposed to tackle these problems by strengthening the role of the Council and giving willing states the opportunity to take the lead in particular areas of cooperation with ENP partners.

There are a number of issues related to the perceptions and visibility of the ENP by the partner countries. The EU is not seen as proposing anything new to its most progressive and committed partners in either the east or the south (e.g. Georgia, Ukraine, Moldova or Tunisia). In particular, the ENP remains reluctant to provide a membership prospect to those EaP states that have concluded association agreements and DCFTAs with the EU and have begun to implement their provisions. Understandably, this contributes to the negative perception about the ENP along with a lack of information in the neighbouring societies about the ENP.

With the aim of improving the perception of the ENP, the 2015 Review pays particular attention to visibility, communication and outreach. In this respect, the EU has declared its intention to intensify its information policy, e.g. by improving public diplomacy, ensuring more open communication about EU projects and allocated funds. The EU also pledges to support the ENP governments and media in reaching a wider public in order to better explain the EU's policies and benefits of cooperation to different segments of their societies. Moreover, it is acknowledged that EU communication activities should also be improved within the Union itself to persuade the EU public of the necessity of continuing cooperation with neighbouring states. The aforementioned steps correspond with the suggestions articulated by experts and scholars in the relevant literature. It is less clear, however, whether those activities will be supported with the necessary commitments of financing and human resources.

The literature analysed in this report is not conclusive on whether the lack of regard for local conditions in the ENP framework is based on the conscious prioritising of EU interests or it is the sheer lack of understanding of what local needs and conditions are in the individual countries. The 2015 Review's increased focus on joint ownership and conscious emphasis on tailoring the policy frameworks promise to move the content of individual partnerships away from being dictated by the EU and thus less EU-centric. The introduction of more individualised assessments of the progress achieved by the ENP countries, introduced by the 2015 Review, is a step not only towards a better assessment of local needs and conditions, but also towards better communication based on shorter, sharper and more political reporting.

Increased emphasis on mutual ownership and tailoring of policies to the needs of individual countries and local conditions constitutes one of the leading themes of the 2015 ENP Review. To this end, the Commission has proposed to initiate consultations with ENP partners concerning "the nature and focus of the partnership" (2015: 4). This report has demonstrated that the lack of clear conceptualisation of such terms as 'partnership' and 'ownership' undermine the process of forming a stronger bond between the EU and the ENP countries and laying the groundwork for effective implementation of the joint ownership principle. The ENP Review addresses the existing concerns over the 'hierarchical' and top-down structure of the EU–ENP countries' relationship and pledges to incorporate shared values, shared interests and the particular needs and concerns voiced by the ENP countries. Still, it does not provide any further clarification on the particular nature of future partnerships.

Going beyond bilateral relations, the Review brings up the need to strengthen the regional dimension of the ENP, as well as create cross-border, interregional and thematic frameworks of cooperation. To some extent, these mirror the recommendations presented by the ENP literature, which argues for more trans-regional cooperation to address the trans-regional external factors influencing the effectiveness of the ENP (Lannon, 2015; Gstöhl, 2015). The emphasis on regional frameworks is furthermore relevant for the impact of the security dimension. Issues such as counter-terrorism require a greater emphasis on trans-regional cooperation and some authors (e.g. Kaunert and Leonard, 2011) have advocated closer coordination between the EU, the ENP countries and external actors.

With regard to the southern dimension of the ENP, the Review notes: "The EU should increase its outreach to partners in sub-Saharan Africa and the Sahel region and in this context ensure coherence with ongoing work on the post-Cotonou agenda" (2015: 19). Reiterating arguments pointing to the high degree of geopolitical interdependencies in the region stretching beyond the southern neighbourhood countries, the increased emphasis on the incorporation of sub-Saharan Africa and the Sahel corresponds with findings and recommendations of the ENP-related research. Nevertheless, the ENP Review lacks detail on this point.

Security remains one of the most pressing concerns of the many neighbourhood countries and the Review incorporates the security dimension within the new ENP. Yet in its current form it only scratches the surface of the issue and is far from meeting the expectations of many ENP countries. As the literature surveyed in this report has shown, there are increasing demands to widen the scope and strengthen the security dimension of the ENP. This is relevant for both the eastern and southern neighbourhoods. The instability in the southern dimension of the ENP as well as the Ukraine crisis and increased assertiveness of Russia have sparked a wave of new concerns over security matters.

Whereas the 2015 Review overlooks the Russian factor, it has dominated the scholarship on the ENP neighbourhood's external actors. And even though the literature extensively discusses the role of Russia in the eastern neighbourhood, no clear consensus exists among scholars on how the EU should proceed vis-à-vis Russia in the context of the ENP and the EaP. The ENP Review does not elaborate on the implications of the deteriorating nature of EU–Russian relations for the ENP in the future. The lack of a consensus on how to deal with Russia is one reason for leaving the Russian factor largely outside of the ENP Review.

For the EU, finding a consensus and acting coherently vis-à-vis the neighbourhood goes beyond its concerns related to Russia. More specifically, both the horizontal and vertical coherence are considered by the literature to be insufficient. Although coherence was addressed in several contributions to the public consultation process, it is clearly not a priority in the new neighbourhood policy. Indeed, the differentiation is likely to have a negative impact on coherence in the ENP. It could be mitigated, however, if the different actors in the EU commit to constructive collaboration. After all, coherence does not mean that the EU should have the same objectives and apply the same policy instruments to all the different ENP countries. As long as each set of objectives and instruments for the individual ENP countries is complementary and mutually reinforcing, coherence in the ENP will be maintained.

Although the Review stresses that the ENP "should be more focused", it remains a very broad policy framework which pursues numerous policy objectives to be realised by various policy instruments. It is therefore remarkable that the Joint Communication does not make a serious attempt to guarantee that the different ENP policy instruments, objectives and actors mutually reinforce each other.

With regard to horizontal coherence, the Joint Communication only mentions that the ENP "will seek to deploy the available instruments and resources in a more coherent and flexible manner". Yet, one of the new key objectives of the ENP Review is joint ownership, which might imply that the EU is less ambitious in promoting its key values to those ENP countries that need them the most. The regimes of those countries prefer the status quo instead of implementing democratic reforms, as the reforms could jeopardise their authority and position.

Another element in the new ENP that can further complicate horizontal coherence is the emphasis on stabilisation. In light of the many conflicts surrounding the EU, the key priority of the ENP is to "comprehensively address sources of instability across sectors". In particular, the new ENP "seeks to offer ways to strengthen the resilience of the EU's partners in the face of external pressures and their ability to make their own sovereign choices". By prioritising stabilisation as an objective of the ENP, there is a serious risk that the 'democratisation-stabilisation dilemma' (identified in the literature) will be amplified. For example, against the background of the stabilisation objective, the Review envisages strengthening cooperation in security sector reform and matters related to the CSDP. At the same time, the Review does not recognise the potential side effects that this capacity-building could entail, such as the consolidation of autocratic leadership. Therefore, the EU should identify clear conditions with regard to good governance, democracy, rule of law and human rights to be met and maintained before engaging in such capacity-building policies.

The need for stronger vertical coherence is also acknowledged in the ENP Review, which states that "the new ENP should be the focus for a more coherent effort by the EU and the member states" and that the "EU is more influential when united in a common approach and communicating a single message". Hence, there will be a greater role for the Council and member states in identifying priorities and in supporting their implementation. Moreover, member states will be invited to play the role of lead partner for certain initiatives or to accompany certain reform efforts. Whereas the Review aims to increase the involvement of the member states in the ENP, it does not specify how vertical coherence can be increased, or in which areas this could be the most useful. Obviously, the EU institutions should remain in the driver's seat in those ENP areas that are implemented as (exclusive) EU policies, such as trade (e.g. the DCFTA) and several areas of sectoral cooperation. Here, flanking measures by member states should operate under the clear guidance of the Council, Commission and/or EEAS. Yet the member states' commitment remains crucial as far as security is concerned. Although the Joint Communication envisages that EU member states will play a more active role in the ENP given the increased level of inter-institutional cooperation, European capitals will not subordinate their national interests to the common EU agenda in the neighbourhood.

This literature review has illustrated that the inter- and intra-intuitional coherence among the different EU institutions is not the most problematic area. Despite some bureaucratic politics, grey areas and 'turf wars', the post-Lisbon architecture functions properly. The EEAS (political aspects), the Commission (trade and sectoral cooperation) and the Council (CFSP/CSDP) cooperate very closely. The ENP Review, however, is likely to make the decision-making process, which is governed mostly by consensus, more difficult. It was easier for the Council to reach an agreement through the one-size-fits-all approach. The implementation of differentiation is expected to be challenging, taking into account the decision-making process through which the individualised partnerships will come into being.

Ultimately, while the 2015 ENP Review is a step forward in its acknowledgement of the deficiencies of the ENP and the main problems that the EU faces in the neighbourhood, it concentrates on handling the current crises but falls short of providing a strategic long-term vision for the EU's relations with its neighbours.

Bibliography

Al-Anani, K., A. Zeidan, M. Cheikh-Rouhou, A. Chickhaoui, A. Driss, M. Elzoughby, M. Kodmani, M. Lahlou and Z. Majed (2011), "The Future of the Mediterranean: Which Way for Europe and North Africa?", Europe in Dialogue 2011/01, Bertelsmann Stiftung, Gütersloh.

Adarov, A., V. Astrov, P. Havlik, G. Hunya, M. Landesmann and L. Podkaminer (2015), "How to Stabilise the Economy of Ukraine", wiiw Background Study No. 201504, Vienna Institute for International Economic Studies, Vienna, April.

Ademmer, E. (2015), "Interdependence and EU-demanded policy change in a shared neighborhood", *Journal of European Public Policy*, Vol. 22, No. 5, pp. 671-689.

Ademmer, E. and L. Delcour (2016), "With a little help from Russia? The European Union and visa liberalization with post-Soviet states", *Eurasian Geography and Economics*, Vol. 57, No. 1, pp. 89-112.

Ademmer, E., L. Delcour and K. Wolczuk (2016), "Beyond geopolitics: Exploring the impact of the EU and Russia in the 'contested neighborhood'", *Eurasian Geography and Economics*, Vol. 57, No. 1, pp. 1-18.

Alieva, L. (2015a), "The European Neighbourhood Policy and Azerbaijan: When Soft Power and Security are Tightly Related", in J. Forbrig and A. Inayeh (ed.), "Reviewing the European Neighbourhood Policy: Eastern Perspectives", Europe Policy Paper No. 4, German Marshall Fund of the United States, Washington, D.C.

Alieva, L. (2015b), "Food-for-thought paper: Azerbaijan", ECFR Riga Series: Views from Eastern Partnership countries, European Council on Foreign Relations.

Astrov, V., P. Havlik, M. Holzner, G. Hunya, I. Mara, S. Richter, R. Stöllinger and H. Vidovic (2012), "European Neighbourhood – Challenges and Opportunities for EU Competitiveness", wiiw Research Report No. 382, Vienna Institute for International Economic Studies, Vienna, September.

Aubert, L. (2011), "The European Union's Policy towards Central Asia and South Caucasus: A Coherent Strategy?", Bruges Regional Integration & Global Governance Papers, 1/2012, College of Europe, Bruges.

Averre, D. (2011), "EU–Russia Relations and the Shared Neighbourhood: An Overview", Directorate-General for External Policies of the Union, European Commission, Brussels.

Babayan, B. (2015), "The return of the empire? Russia's counteraction to transatlantic democracy promotion in its near abroad", *Democratization*, Vol. 22, No. 3, pp. 438-458.

Balfour, R. (2012a), "EU Conditionality after the Arab Spring", IEMed Euromesco series, No. 16, European Institute of the Mediterranean, Barcelona, June.

Balfour, R. (2012b), *Human Rights and Democracy in EU Foreign Policy: The Cases of Ukraine and Egypt,* London: Routledge.

Balfour, R. (2015), "Making the Most of the European Neighbourhood Policy Toolbox", Blog Post, German Marshall Fund of the United States, Washington, D.C., 18 November.

Balfour, R. (2016), "The European Neighbourhood Policy's Identity Crisis", Euromed Survey No. 6: Qualitative Analysis, European Institute of the Mediterranean, Barcelona.

Bello, O. (2012), "Quick Fix or Quicksand? Implementing the EU Sahel Strategy", Working Paper No. 114, FRIDE, Madrid.

Benedyczak, J., L. Litra and K. Mrozek (2015), "Moldova's success story: The visa-free regime with the EU one year on", Stefan Batory Foundation, Warsaw.

Berg, E. (2014), "Do They Really Have a Choice? Eastern Partnership States between the EU and Russia", in PONARS Eurasia (ed.), *The Vilnius Moment*, 1st edition, PONARS Eurasia, George Washington University, Washington, D.C., pp. 1-5.

Bicchi, F. (2014), "Information exchanges, diplomatic networks and the construction of European knowledge in European Union foreign policy", *Cooperation and Conflict*, Vol. 49, No. 2, pp. 239-259.

Biscop, S. (2016), "Geopolitics with European Characteristics: An Essay on Pragmatic Idealism, Equality, and Strategy", Egmont Paper No. 82, Egmont Institute, Brussels, March, pp. 1- 29.

Biscop, S., R. Balfour and M. Emerson (2012), "An Arab Springboard for EU Foreign Policy?", Egmont Paper No. 54, Egmont Institute, Brussels.

Blockmans, S. (2015), "The 2015 ENP Review: A policy in suspended animation", CEPS Commentary, Centre for European Policy Studies, Brussels, 1 December.

Blockmans, S. (2016a), "New Thrust for the CSDP from the Refugee and Migrant Crisis", CEPS Special Report, Centre for European Policy Studies, Brussels.

Blockmans, S. (2016b), "Can the EU help prevent further conflict in Iraq and Syria?", CEPS Commentary, Centre for European Policy Studies, Brussels, 25 November.

Blockmans, S., A. Ehteshami and G. Bahgat (eds) (2016), *EU–Iran Relations after the Nuclear Deal*, CEPS e-Book, Centre for European Policy Studies, Brussels, February.

Blockmans, S. and C. Hillion (eds) (2013a), "EEAS 2.0: A legal commentary on Council Decision 2010/427/EU establishing the organisation and functioning of the European External Action Service", Working Paper No. 99, Leuven Center for Global Governance Studies, KU Leuven, February.

Blockmans, S. and C. Hillion (eds) (2013b), "EEAS 2.0: Recommendations for the amendment of Council Decision 2010/427/EU establishing the organisation and functioning of the European External Action Service", CEPS Special Report No. 78, Centre for European Policy Studies, Brussels, 13 November.

Blockmans, S. and B. Van Vooren (2012), "Revitalizing the European 'Neighbourhood Economic Community': The Case for Legally Binding Sectoral Multilateralism", *European Foreign Affairs Review*, Vol. 17, No. 4, pp. 577-604.

Blockmans S., H. Kostanyan and I. Vorobiov (2012), "Towards a Eurasian Economic Union: The challenge of integration and unity", CEPS Special Report No. 75, Centre for European Policy Studies, Brussels, December.

Bodenstein, T. and M. Furness (2009), "Separating the Willing from the Able: Is the European Union's Mediterranean Policy Incentive Compatible?", *European Union Politics*, Vol. 10, No. 3, pp. 381-401.

Boiten, V.J. (2015), "The Semantics of 'Civil': The EU, Civil Society and the Building of Democracy in Tunisia", *European Foreign Affairs Review*, Vol. 20, No. 3, pp. 357–378.

Boogaerts, A., C. Portela and E. Drieskens (2016), "One Swallow Does Not Make Spring: A Critical Juncture Perspective on the EU Sanctions in Response to the Arab Spring", *Mediterranean Politics*, Vol. 12, No. 2.

Bonavita, V. (2015), "The externalisation of border controls towards the EU's broader neighbourhood: Challenges and consistency", in S. Gstöhl and E. Lannon (eds), *The European Union's broader neighbourhood: Challenges and opportunities for cooperation beyond the European Neighbourhood Policy*, London and New York: Routledge, pp. 11-36.

Bond, I. (2014), "The EU and Russia: Uncommon Spaces", Centre for European Reform, London.

Bond, I., C. Odendahl and J. Rankin (2015), "Frozen: the politics and economics of sanctions against Russia", Centre for European Reform, London.

Börzel, T.A. and V. van Hüllen (2014), "One voice, one message, but conflicting goals: Cohesiveness and consistency in the European Neighbourhood Policy", *Journal of European Public Policy*, Vol. 21, No. 7, pp. 1033-1049.

Börzel, T.A. and B. Lebanidze (2015), "European Neighbourhood Policy at the Crossroads Evaluating the Past to Shape the Future", MAXCAP Working Paper No. 12, Maximizing the integration capacity of the European Union: Lessons of and prospects for enlargement and beyond (MAXCAP Project), July.

Bosse, G. (2016), "Markets versus Morals? Assessing EU Arms Exports to Autocratic Regimes in its Closer and Wider Neighbourhood", in S. Gstöhl (ed.), *The European Neighbourhood Policy in a Comparative Perspective*, Farnham: Ashgate.

Bouris, D. and T. Schumacher (eds) (2016), *The Revised European Neighbourhood Policy: Continuity and Change in EU Foreign Policy*, Basingstoke: Palgrave Macmillan.

Bower, A. and R. Metais (2015), "State of Play: The EU, the Arabian Peninsula, Iraq, Iran and the ENP", in S. Gstöhl and E. Lannon (eds), *The neighbours of the European Union's neighbours: Diplomatic and geopolitical dimensions beyond the European neighbourhood policy*, 1st edition, Farnham: Ashgate Publishing Ltd.

Buras, P. (2015), "Poland and the Eastern Partnership: The view from Warsaw", ECFR Riga Series: Views from the EU, European Council on Foreign Relations, pp. 30-33.

Buscaneanu, S. (2012), "EU Democracy Promotion in Eastern ENP Countries", *East European Politics and Societies*, Vol. 29, No. 1, pp. 248-268.

Buschle, D. (2014), "Exporting the Internal Market – Panacea or Nemesis for the European Neighbourhood Policy? Lessons from the Energy Community", EU Diplomacy Paper No. 2/2014, College of Europe, Bruges.

Buzogány, A. (2016), "EU-Russia regulatory competition and business interests in post-Soviet countries: The case of forestry and chemical security in Ukraine", *Eurasian Geography and Economics*, Vol. 57, No. 1, pp. 138-159.

Cadier, D. (2013), "Is the European Neighbourhood Policy a substitute for enlargement?", in *The Crisis of EU Enlargement*, LSE IDEAS Special Report, LSE IDEAS, London, November.

Casier, T. (2011), "The EU's two-track approach to democracy promotion: The case of Ukraine", *Democratization*, Vol. 18, No. 4, pp. 956-977.

Cassarino, J.P. (2014), "Channelled Policy Transfers: EU-Tunisia Interactions on Migration Matters", *European Journal of Migration and Law*, Vol. 16, No. 1, pp. 97-12.

Cebeci, M. (2016), "Deconstructing the 'ideal power Europe' meta-narrative in the revised European Neighbourhood Policy", in D. Bouris and T. Schumacher (eds), *The Revised European Neighbourhood Policy: Continuity and Change in EU Foreign Policy*, Basingstoke: Palgrave Macmillan, pp. 57-76.

Chamon, M. (2016), *EU agencies: Legal and political limits to the transformation of the EU administration*, Oxford: Oxford University Press.

Charokopos, M. (2013), "Energy Community and European Common Aviation Area: Two tales of one story", *European Foreign Affairs Review*, Vol. 18, No. 2, pp. 273-296.

Cohen-Hadria, E. (2016), "EU Member States and the ENP: Towards Greater Ownership?", Euromed Survey No. 6, European Institute of the Mediterranean, Barcelona.

Comelli, M. (2013), "Potential and Limits of EU Policies in the Neighbourhood", Policy Paper, No. 68, Notre Europe-Jacques Delors Institute, Paris and Berlin, February.

Cooley, A. (2015), "Countering Democratic Norms", *Journal of Democracy*, Vol. 26, No. 3, July, pp. 49-63.

Connolly, R. (2015), "Troubled Times Stagnation, Sanctions and the Prospects for Economic Reform in Russia", Chatham House Research Paper, London, February.

Cremona, M. (2011), "Values in EU Foreign Policy", in M. Evans and P. Koutrakos (eds), *Beyond the Established Orders: Policy Interconnections between the EU and the Rest of the World*, Oxford: Hart Publishing, pp. 275-315.

Ćwiek-Karpowicz, J. and S. Secrieru (eds) (2015), "Sanctions and Russia", Polish Institute of International Affairs, Warsaw.

Dabrowski, M. (2014), "Ukraine: Can Meaningful Reform come out of Conflict?", Bruegel Policy Contribution, Issue 8, Brussels, July.

Dandashly, A. (2015), "The EU Response to Regime Change in the Wake of the Arab Revolt: Differential Implementation", *Journal of European Integration*, Vol. 37, No. 1, pp. 37-56.

Dashwood, A., M. Dougan, B. Rodger, E. Spaventa and D. Derrick Wyatt (2011), *Wyatt and Dashwood's European Union Law*, 6th edition, Oxford: Hart Publishing.

Delcour, L. (2015a), "In Need of a New Paradigm? Rethinking the European Neighbourhood Policy/Eastern Partnership", Eastern Partnership Review No. 20, Estonian Center of Eastern Partnership, Tallinn, April.

Delcour, L. (2015b), "The 2015 ENP Review: Beyond Stocktaking, the Need for a Political Strategy", CEBOP No. 1.15, College of Europe, Bruges, December.

Delcour, L. (2016a), "Multiple external influences and domestic change in the contested neighborhood: The case of food safety", *Eurasian Geography and Economics*, Vol. 57, No. 1, pp. 43-65.

Delcour, L. (2016b), "Conclusions: Plus ça change, plus c'est la même chose? The European Neighbourhood Policy and Dynamics of Internal and External Change", in D. Bouris and T. Schumacher (eds), *The Revised European Neighbourhood Policy: Continuity and Change in EU Foreign Policy*, Basingstoke: Palgrave Macmillan, pp. 285-297.

Delcour, L. and H. Kostanyan (2014), "Towards a Fragmented Neighbourhood: Policies of the EU and Russia and their consequences for the area that lies in between", CEPS Essay No. 17, Centre for European Policy Studies, Brussels, October.

Delcour, L. and K. Wolczuk (2013a), "Approximation of the national legislation of Eastern Partnership countries with EU legislation in the economic field", Study, DG for External Policies of the Union, European Parliament, May.

Delcour, L. and K. Wolczuk (2013b), "Beyond the Vilnius Summit: Challenges for Deeper EU Integration with Eastern Europe", Policy Brief, European Policy Centre, Brussels, October.

Delcour, L., H. Kostanyan, B. Vandecasteele and P. Van Elsuwege (2015), "The implications of Eurasian integration for the EU's relations with the countries in the post-Soviet space", *Studia Diplomatica*, Vol. 68, No. 1, pp. 5-33.

Del Sarto, R.A. and T. Schumacher (2011), "From Brussels with love: Leverage, benchmarking, and the action plans with Jordan and Tunisia in the EU's democratization policy", *Democratization*, Vol. 18, No. 4, pp. 932-955.

Dennison, S. and A. Dworkin (2011), "Europe and the Arab Revolution: A New Vision for Democracy and Human Rights", ECFR Policy Brief, European Council on Foreign Relations, November.

Dennison, S., A. Dworkin, N. Popescu and N. Witney (2011), "After the Revolution: Europe and the Transition in Tunisia", Policy Brief, European Council on Foreign Relations.

Dias, V.A. (2014), "A critical analysis of the EU's response to the Arab spring and its implications for EU security", *Human Security Perspectives*, Vol. 10, No. 1, pp. 26–61.

Dimitrova, A. and R. Dragneva (2013), "Shaping Convergence with the EU in Foreign Policy and State Aid in Post-Orange Ukraine: Weak External Incentives, Powerful Veto Players", *Europe-Asia Studies*, Vol. 65, No. 4, pp. 658-681.

Dolidze, T. (2015), "EU Sanctions Policy towards Russia: The Sanctioner–Sanctionee's Game of Thrones", CEPS Working Document No. 402, Centre for European Policy Studies, Brussels, January.

Dostál, V., N. Karasova and V. Lidl (2015), "Trends of Eastern Partnership", Association for International Affairs, Prague.

Dragneva, R. and K. Wolczuk (2013), *Eurasian Economic Integration: Law, Policy and Politics*, Cheltenham: Edward Elgar.

Dragneva, R. and K. Wolczuk (2014), "The EU-Ukraine Association Agreement and the Challenges of Inter-regionalism", *Review of Central and East European Law*, Vol. 39, Nos 3-4, pp. 213-244.

Dragneva, R. and K. Wolczuk (2015), *Ukraine between the EU and Russia: The Integration Challenge*, Basingstoke: Palgrave Macmillan.

Dreger, C., K.A. Kholodilin, D. Ulbricht and J. Fidrmuc (2016), "Between the hammer and the anvil: The impact of economic sanctions and oil prices on Russia's ruble", *Journal of Comparative Economics*, Vol. 44, No. 2, pp. 295–308.

Duleba, A., V. Benč and V. Bilčík (2012), "Policy Impact of the Eastern Partnership on Ukraine: Trade, Energy, and Visa Dialogue", Research Center of the Slovak Foreign Policy Association, Bratislava.

Dumas, P. and I. Lang (2015), "EU Mobility Regimes and Visa Policy towards ENP Countries", EUI Working Paper No. 79, Robert Schuman Centre for Advanced Studies Migration Policy Centre, Florence.

Dworkin, A. and F. Wesslau (2015), "Ten talking points from the new ENP", Commentary, European Council on Foreign Relations, Brussels, 20 November.

Echagüe, A. (2012), "Don't Forget the Gulf", in K. Kausch and R. Youngs (eds), *Europe in the Reshaped Middle East*, 1st edition, FRIDE, Madrid, pp. 35-45.

Ecorys and CASE (2012), "Trade Sustainability Impact Assessment in support of negotiations of a DCFTA between the EU and Georgia and the Republic of Moldova", Rotterdam, 27 October.

Eisele, K. and A. Wiesbrock (2011), "Enhancing Mobility in the European Neighborhood Policy? The Cases of Moldova and Georgia", *Review of Central and East European Law*, Vol. 36, No. 2, pp. 127-155.

Emerson, M. (2011), "Review of the Review – of the European Neighbourhood Policy", CEPS Commentary, Centre for European Policy Studies, Brussels, 8 June.

Emerson, M. and H. Kostanyan (2013), "Putin's grand design to destroy the EU's Eastern Partnership and replace it with a disastrous neighbourhood policy of his own", CEPS Commentary, Centre for European Policy Studies, Brussels, 17 September.

Emerson, M., V. Movchan, S. Blockmans, H. Kostanyan, G. Van der Loo, O. Betliy, K. Furmanets, I. Kosse, O. Krasovska, K. Kravchuk, V. Kravchuk, Y. Oharenko, M. Ryzhenkov and O. Stepanyuk (2016a), *Deepening EU-Ukraine Relations: What, Why and How*, CEPS Paperback, London: Rowman & Littlefield International.

Emerson, M., D. Cenusa, S. Blockmans, H. Kostanyan, G. Van der Loo, V. Gumene, I. Morcotylo, D. Pîntea and A. Popa (2016b), *Deepening EU-Moldova Relations: What, Why and How*, CEPS Paperback, London: Rowman & Littlefield International.

Emerson, M., T. Kovziridze, S. Blockmans, H. Kostanyan, G. Van der Loo, G. Akhalaia, D. Bolkvadze, Z. Chelidze, G. Duduchava, L. Gogoberidze, A. Kacharava, H. Khoshtaria, V. Lejava, N. Samushia and G. Zedginidze (2016c), *Deepening EU-Georgia Relations: What, Why and How*, CEPS Paperback, London: Rowman & Littlefield International.

European Commission (2004), "European Neighbourhood Strategy Paper", COM(2004) 373 Final, Brussels, 12 May.

European Commission and High Representative (2011), Joint Communication to the European Parliament, the Council, the European Economic and Social Committee and the Committee of the Regions, "A New Response to the Changing Neighbourhood", COM(2011) 303, Brussels, 25 May.

European Commission and High Representative (2015), Joint Communication to the European Parliament, the Council, the European Economic and Social Committee and the Committee of the Regions, "Review of the European Neighbourhood Policy", JOIN(2015) 50 final, Brussels, 17 November.

European Council on Foreign Relations (ECFR) (2015), *ECFR Riga Series: Views from EaP countries*, ECFR.

Faleg, G. and S. Blockmans (2016), "EU Naval Force EUNAVFOR MED sets sail in troubled waters", CEPS Commentary, Centre for European Policy Studies, Brussels, 26 June.

Falkenhain, M. and I. Solonenko (2012), "The EU an in Morocco" in K. Böttger and T.A. Börzel (eds), *Policy Change in the EU's Immediate Neighbourhood: A Sectoral Approach*, Baden-Baden: Nomos, 56-76.

Fernández, H.A. and T. Behr (2013), *The Missing Spring in the EU's Mediterranean Policies*, Notre Europe Policy Paper, No. 70, Jacques Delors Institut, Berlin, February.

Filippos, P. (2016), "EU Energy Security beyond Ukraine: Towards Holistic Diversification", *European Foreign Affairs Review*, Vol. 21, No. 1, pp. 57–74.

Fischer, S. (2012), "The European Union and the Insiders/Outsiders of Europe: Russia and the Post-Soviet Space", *Review of European Studies*, Vol. 4, No. 3.

Franceson, S. (2015), "Italy and the Eastern Partnership: The view from Rome", Commentary, ECFR Riga Series: Views from the EU, European Council on Foreign Relations, pp. 8-10.

Freizer, S. (2016), "The Revised European Neighbourhood Policy and Conflicts in the South Caucasus: The EU's Growing Conflict Transformation Role", in D. Bouris and T. Schumacher (eds), *The Revised European Neighbourhood Policy: Continuity and Change in EU Foreign Policy*, Basingstoke: Palgrave Macmillan, pp. 157-176.

Freyburg, T. (2012), "The two sides of functional cooperation with authoritarian regimes: A multi-level perspective on the conflict of objectives between political stability and democratic change", *Democratization*, Vol. 19, No. 3, pp. 575-601.

Freyburg, T. and S. Richter (2015), "Local actors in the driver's seat: Transatlantic democracy promotion under regime competition in the Arab world", *Democratization*, Vol. 22, No. 3, pp. 496-518.

Freyburg, T., S. Lavenex, F. Schimmelfennig, T. Skripka and A. Wetzel (2011), "Democracy promotion through functional cooperation? The case of the European Neighbourhood Policy", *Democratization*, Vol. 8 No. 4, pp. 1026-1054.

Freyburg, T., S. Lavenex, F. Schimmelfennig, T. Skripka and A. Wetzel (2015), *Democracy promotion by functional cooperation*, 1st edition, London: Palgrave Macmillan.

Gaub, F. and N. Popescu (2015), "The EU Neighbours 1995-2015: Shades of Grey", EUISS, Chaillot Paper No. 136, EU Institute for Security Studies, Paris, December.

Gebhard, C. (2011), "Coherence", in C. Hill and M. Smith (eds), *International Relations and the European Union*, Oxford: Oxford University Press, pp. 101-127.

Ghazaryan, N. (2014), *The European Neighbourhood Policy and the Democratic Values of the EU: A Legal Analysis*, Oxford: Hart Publishing.

Ghazaryan, N. (2016), "The Fluid Concept of 'EU values' in the Neighbourhood: A Change of Paradigm from East to South?", in S. Poli (ed.), *The European Neighbourhood Policy – Values and Principles*, Abingdon: Routledge, pp. 11-32.

Giragosian, R. (2015a), "The European Neighbourhood Policy: An Armenian Perspective", in J. Forbrig and A. Inayeh (ed.), "Reviewing the European Neighbourhood Policy: Eastern Perspectives", Europe Policy Paper No. 4, German Marshall Fund of the United States, Washington, D.C.

Giragosian, R. (2015b), "Food-for-thought paper: Armenia", ECFR Riga Series: Views from EaP countries, European Council on Foreign Relations.

Giumelli, F. (2011), "EU Restrictive Measures on the Transnistrian Leaders: Assessing Effectiveness in a Strategy of Divide and Influence", *European Foreign Affairs Review*, Vol. 16, No. 3, pp. 359-378.

Giumelli, F. (2013), "How EU sanctions work: A new narrative", EUISS Chaillot Paper, No. 129, EU Institute for Security Studies, Paris, May.

Giusti, S. (2016), "The EU's Transformative Power Challenged in Ukraine", *European Foreign Affairs Review*, Vol. 21, No. 2, pp. 165-184.

Gligorov, V., P. Havlik, S. Richter and H. Vidovic (2012), "Transition in the MENA Region: Challenges, Opportunities and Prospects", wiiw Research Report No. 376, Institute for International Economic Studies, Vienna, January.

Grant, C. (2011), "A New Neighbourhood Policy for the EU", CER Policy Brief, Centre for European Reform, London, March.

Gressel, G. (2016), "Keeping up Appearances: How Europe is Supporting Ukraine's Transformation", European Council on Foreign Relations, October.

Grevi, G. (2014), "Re-defining the EU's neighbourhood", in G. Grevi and D. Keohane (eds), *Challenges for European Foreign Policy in 2014*, 1st edition, FRIDE, Madrid, pp. 15-22.

Grimm, S. and J. Leininger (2012), "Not all good things go together: Conflicting objectives in democracy promotion", *Democratization*, Vol. 19, No. 3, pp. 391-414.

Gros, D. and F. Mustilli (2015), "The Economic Impact of Sanctions against Russia: Much ado about very little", CEPS Commentary, Centre for European Policy Studies, Brussels, October.

Gstöhl, S. (2015), "Conclusion: Models of Cooperation with the Neighbours of the EU's Neighbours", in S. Gstöhl and E. Lannon (eds), *The neighbours of the European Union's neighbours: Diplomatic and geopolitical dimensions beyond the European neighbourhood policy*, 1st edition, Farnham: Ashgate Publishing Ltd.

Gstöhl, S. (2016a), *The European Neighbourhood Policy in a comparative perspective: Models, challenges, lessons*, Abingdon: Routledge.

Gstöhl, S. (2016b), "The Contestation of Values in the European Neighbourhood Policy: Challenges of Capacity, Consistency and Competition", in S. Poli (ed.), *The European Neighbourhood Policy – Values and Principles*, Abingdon: Routledge, pp. 58-78.

Gstöhl, S. and E. Lannon (2015), *The neighbours of the European Union's neighbours: Diplomatic and geopolitical dimensions beyond the European neighbourhood policy*, 1st edition, Farnham: Ashgate Publishing Ltd.

Gstöhl, S. and S. Schunz (eds) (2016), *Theorizing the European Neighbourhood Policy*, London and New York: Routledge.

Guild, E. and S. Carrera (2016), "Rethinking asylum distribution in the EU: Shall we start with the facts?", CEPS Commentary, Centre for European Policy Studies, Brussels, 17 June.

Hale, J. (2012), "EU relations with Azerbaijan: More for Less?", Discussion Paper, Open Society European Policy Institute, Brussels.

Hallgren, H. and I. Sololenko (2015), "Can the European Union Help Ukraine to Succeed? Reforms, the Russian Factor and Implications for the Eastern Neighbourhood", Heinrich Böll Stiftung European Union, Brussels.

Halubnichy, D. (2015), "Food-for-thought paper: Belarus", ECFR Riga Series: Views from EaP countries, European Council on Foreign Relations.

Harpaz, G. (2014), "Approximation of Laws under the European Neighbourhood Policy: The Challenges that Lie Ahead", *European Foreign Affairs Review*, Vol. 19, No. 3, pp. 429-452.

Hassan, O. (2015), "Undermining the transatlantic democracy agenda? The Arab Spring and Saudi Arabia's counteracting democracy strategy", *Democratization*, Vol., 22, No. 3, pp. 479-495.

Hasanov, R. (2015), "Position Paper 2: Azerbaijan", in F. Hett, S. Kikić and S. Meuser (eds), *Reassessing the European Neighbourhood Policy: The Eastern Dimension*, Friedrich-Ebert-Stiftung, Berlin, June.

Haukkala, H. (2016), "The EU's regional normative hegemony encounters hard realities: The revised European Neighbourhood Policy and the ring of fire", in D. Bouris and T. Schumacher (eds), *The Revised European Neighbourhood Policy: Continuity and Change in EU Foreign Policy*, Basingstoke: Palgrave Macmillan.

Havlik, P. (2014), "Economic Consequences of the Ukraine Conflict", wiiw Policy Note/Policy Report No. 14, Vienna Institute for International Economic Studies, Vienna, November.

Helwig, N., P. Ivan and H. Kostanyan (2013), *The New EU Foreign Policy Architecture: Reviewing the first two years of EEAS*, CEPS e-Book, Centre for European Policy Studies, Brussels.

Henökl, T. and A. Stemberger (2016), "EU Policies in the Arab World: Update and Critical Assessment", *European Foreign Affairs Review*, Vol. 21, No. 2, pp. 227–250.

Hertog, L. and S. Stross (2013), "Coherence in EU External Relations: Concepts and Legal Rooting of an Ambiguous Term", *European Foreign Affairs Review*, Vol. 18, No. 3, pp. 373-388.

Hett, F., A. Kellner and B. Martin (2014), "The EU and the East in 2030: Four Scenarios for Relations between the EU, the Russian Federation, and the Common Neighbourhood", Friedrich-Ebert-Stiftung, Berlin.

Hillion, C. (2013), "The EU Neighbourhood Competences under Article 8 TEU", Policy Paper No. 69, Notre Europe–Jacques Delors Institute, Paris and Berlin, February.

Hillion, C. (2014), "Anatomy of EU norm export to the neighbourhood: The impact of Article 8 TEU", in P. Van Elsuwege and R. Petrov (eds), *Legislative Approximation and Application of EU Law in the Eastern Neighbourhood of the European Union: Towards a Common Regulatory Space?*, Abingdon: Routledge, pp. 13-20.

Hollis, R. (2012), "No friend of democratization: Europe's role in the genesis of the Arab Spring", *International Affairs*, Vol. 88, No. 1, pp. 81-101.

IEMed (2016), *European Neighbourhood Policy Review: European Union's Role in the Mediterranean*, Euromed Survey No. 6: Descriptive Report, European Institute of the Mediterranean, Barcelona.

Inayeh, A. and J. Forbrig (eds) (2015), "Reviewing the European Neighbourhood Policy: Eastern Perspectives", GMF Europe Policy Paper No. 4, German Marshall Fund of the United States, Washington, D.C.

Johnston, C. (2015), "Sanctions against Russia: Evasion, Compensation and Overcompliance", EUISS Brief No. 13, EU Institute for Security Studies, Paris, May.

Jonasson, A.K. (2013), *The EU's Democracy Promotion and the Mediterranean Neighbors: Orientation, Ownership and Dialogue in Jordan and Turkey*, Abingdon: Routledge.

Jünemann, A. (2012), "Civil Society, Its Role and Potential in the New Mediterranean Context: Which EU Policies?", IEMed Obs Focus Article No. 86/5, European Observatory of Euro-Mediterranean Policies, Barcelona.

Kaca, E., A. Sobják and K. Zasztowt (2014), *Learning from Past Experiences: Ways to Improve EU Aid on Reforms in the Eastern Partnership*, PISM Report, Polish Institute of International Affairs, Warsaw, April.

Kałan, D. (2013), "East of Centre: Can the Visegrad Group Speak with One Voice on Eastern Policy?", PISM Policy Paper No. 5 (53), Polish Institute of International Affairs, Warsaw, February.

Kaminska, J. (2016), "The European Parliament and the revised European Neighbourhood Policy", in D. Bouris and T. Schumacher (eds), *The Revised European Neighbourhood Policy: Continuity and Change in EU Foreign Policy*, Basingstoke: Palgrave Macmillan, pp. 135-154.

Kanet, R.E. and M. Raquel Freire (eds) (2012), *Competing for Influence: The EU and Russia in Post-Soviet Eurasia*, Dordrecht: Republic of Letters Publishing BV.

Kasčiūnas, L., V. Keršanskas, K. Vaičiūnaitė and B. Balázs Jarábik (2013), "Eastern Partnership after Vilnius: A Mission Accomplished, Mounting Tasks Ahead", Eastern Europe Studies Center, Vilnius, November.

Kasčiūnas, L., V. Ivanauskas, V. Keršanskas and L. Kojala (2014), "Eastern Partnership in a Changed Security Environment: New Incentives for Reform", Eastern Europe Studies Centre, Vilnius, November.

Kaunert, C. and S. Léonard (2011), "EU Counterterrorism and the European Neighbourhood Policy: An Appraisal of the Southern Dimension", *Terrorism and Political Violence*, Vol. 23, No. 2, pp. 286-309.

Kausch, K. (2013), "The End of the (Southern) Neighbourhood", IEMed Euromesco series, No. 18, European Institute of the Mediterranean, Barcelona, April.

Kausch, K. and R. Youngs (eds) (2012), *Europe in the Reshaped Middle East*, FRIDE, Madrid.

Keukeleire, S. (2015), "Lessons for the practice and analysis of EU diplomacy from an 'outside-in' perspective", in S. Gstöhl and E. Lannon (eds), *The Neighbours of the European Union's Neighbours: Diplomatic and Geopolitical Dimensions beyond the European Neighbourhood Policy*, 1st edition, Farnham: Ashgate Publishing Ltd.

Khalifa Isaac, S. (2013), "Rethinking the New ENP: A Vision for an Enhanced European Role in the Arab Revolutions", *Democracy and Security*, Vol. 9, Nos 1-2, pp. 40-60.

Kimber, A. and E. Halliste (2015), "EU-related Communication in Eastern Partnership Countries", Eastern Partnership Review No. 25, Estonian Center of Eastern Partnership, Tallinn, May, pp. 1-36.

Kirova, I. and S. Freizer (2015), "Civil Society Voices: How the EU Should Engage its Eastern Neighbours", Briefing Paper, Open Society European Policy Institute, Brussels, May.

Kobzova, J. (2015), "Eastern Partnership after Riga: Rethink, reforms, resilience", ECFR Commentary, European Council on Foreign Relations, May.

Kobzova, J. and L. Alieva (2012), "The EU and Azerbaijan: Beyond Oil", ECFR Commentary, European Council on Foreign Relations, May.

Kochenov, D. and E. Basheska (2015), "ENP's Value Conditionality: From Enlargements to Post-Crimea", CLEER Paper No. 1, Centre for the Law of EU External Relations, The Hague.

Koenig, N. (2011), "The EU and the Libyan Crisis: In Quest for Coherence?", IAI Working Paper No. 11/19, Istituto Affari Internazionali, Rome, July.

Koenig, N. (2013), "The EU and the Libyan Crisis: In Quest of Coherence?", IAI Working Paper No. 11, Istituto Affari Internazionali, Rome, July.

Koenig, N. (2016), "Taking the European Neighbourhood Policy beyond the Conception-performance Gap", Policy Paper No. 160, Jacques Delors Institut, Berlin, March.

Korosteleva, E. (2011), "Change or Continuity: Is the Eastern Partnership an Adequate Tool for the European Neighbourhood?", *International Relations*, Vol. 25, No. 2, pp. 243-262.

Korosteleva, E. (2012), *The European Union and its Eastern Neighbours: Towards a more ambitious partnership?*, London and New York: Routledge.

Korosteleva, E. (2013), "Evaluating the role of partnership in the European Neighbourhood Policy: The Eastern neighbourhood", *Eastern Journal of European Studies*, Vol. 4, No. 3, pp. 11-36.

Korosteleva, E. (2016a), "EU-Russia relations in the context of the eastern neighbourhood", Policy Brief, Bertelsmann Stiftung, Gütersloh, May.

Korosteleva, E. (2016b), "The European Union, Russia and the Eastern region: The analytics of government for sustainable cohabitation", *Cooperation and Conflict*, Vol. 51, No. 3, pp. 365-383.

Korosteleva, E. (2016c), "The EU and Belarus: Seizing the Opportunity?", European Policy Analysis No. 13, Swedish Institute for European Policy Studies, Stockholm, November.

Kostanyan, H. (2013), "The EEAS and the European neighbourhood policy: A change in rhetoric or reality?", CIES Neighbourhood Policy Paper No. 9, Centre for European and International Studies, Istanbul, pp. 1-8.

Kostanyan, H. (2014a), "Examining the discretion of the EEAS: What power to act in the EU– Moldova association agreement?", European Foreign Affairs Review, Vol. 19, No. 3, pp. 373-392.

Kostanyan, H. (2014b), "The Civil Society Forum of the Eastern Partnership: Four Years on Progress, Challenges and Prospects", CEPS Special Report, Centre for European Policy Studies, Brussels.

Kostanyan, H. (2015), "The Rocky Road to and EU–Armenia Agreement: From U-turn to detour", CEPS Commentary, Centre for European Policy Studies, Brussels, 3 February.

Kostanyan, H. (2016a), "The EEAS and the revised European Neighbourhood Policy: What institutional balance?", in D. Bouris and T. Schumacher (eds), The Revised European Neighbourhood Policy: Continuity and Change in EU Foreign Policy, Basingstoke: Palgrave Macmillan, pp. 117-134.

Kostanyan, H. (2016b), "The European Neighbourhood Policy reviewed: Shifting from value- driven to classical foreign policy", in A. Hug (ed.), Institutionally blind? International organisations and human rights abuses in the former Soviet Union, Foreign Policy Centre, London, pp. 17-21.

Kostanyan, H. and B. Vandecasteele (2013), "The EuroNest Parliamentary Assembly: The European Parliament as a Socializer of its Counterparts in the EU's Eastern Neighbourhood?", EU Diplomacy Paper No. 5, College of Europe, Bruges.

Kostanyan, H. and B. Vandecasteele (2015), "Socializing the Eastern neighbourhood: The European Parliament and the EuroNest Parliamentary Assembly", in S. Stavridis and D. Irrera, (eds), The European Parliament and its International Relations, London: Routledge, pp. 220-233.

Kostanyan, H. and J. Orbie, J. (2013), "The EEAS' discretionary power within the Eastern Partnership: In search of the highest possible denominator", *Journal of Southeast European and Black Sea Studies*, Vol. 13, No. 1, pp. 47–65.

Kostanyan, H. and M. Nasieniak (2012), "Moving the EU from a Laggard to a Leader in Democracy Assistance: The Potential Role of the European Endowment for Democracy", CEPS Policy Brief No. 273, Centre for European Policy Studies, Brussels.

Kostanyan, H. and R. Giragosian (2016), "Seizing the Second Chance in EU-Armenia Relations", CEPS Commentary, Centre for European Policy Studies, Brussels, 31 October.

Kostanyan, H. and S. Meister (2016), "Ukraine, Russia and the EU: Breaking the deadlock in the Minsk process", CEPS Working Document No. 423, Centre for European Policy Studies, Brussels, June.

Kurki, M. (2012), "How the EU can Adopt a new Type of Democracy Support", FRIDE Working Paper No. 112, FRIDE, Madrid, March.

Langbein, J. (2013), "Unpacking the Russian and EU Impact on Policy Change in the Eastern Neighbourhood: The Case of Ukraine's Telecommunications and Food Safety", *Europe-Asia Studies*, Vol. 65, No. 4, pp. 631-657.

Langbein, J. and K. Wolczuk (2012), "Convergence without membership? The impact of the European Union in the neighbourhood: Evidence from Ukraine", *Journal of European Public Policy*, Vol. 19, No. 6, pp. 863-881.

Langbein, J. and T.A. Börzel (2013), "Explaining Policy Change in the European Union's Eastern Neighbourhood", *Europe-Asia Studies*, Vol. 65, No. 4, pp. 571-580.

Lannon, E. (2014), "An economic response to the crisis: Towards a new generation of deep and comprehensive free trade areas with the Mediterranean partner countries", European Parliament Studies, Policy Department Workshop on "The Euromed Region after the Arab Spring and the New Generation of DCFTAs" held on 18 June, Brussels.

Lannon, E. (2015), "More for more or less for less: From the rhetoric to the implementation of European Neighbourhood Instrument in the Context of the 2015 ENP review", IEMed Overview, European Institute of the Mediterranean, Barcelona, pp. 220-224.

Larsen, H. (2014), "The EU as a Normative Power and the Research on External Perceptions: The Missing Link", *Journal of Common Market Studies*, Vol. 52, No. 4, pp. 896-910.

Laruelle, M., P. Krekó, L. Győri, D. Haller and R. Reichstadt (2015), "From Paris to Vladivostok: The Kremlin connections of the French far-right", Political Capital Institute, Budapest, December.

Lavenex, S. and F. Schimmelfennig (2011), "EU democracy promotion in the neighbourhood: From leverage to governance?", *Democratization*, Vol. 18, No. 4, pp. 885-909.

Lavenex, S. and F. Schimmelfennig (2013), *Democracy promotion in the EU's Neighbourhood: From leverage to governance?*, Abingdon: Routledge

Lebduška, M. and V. Lídl (2014), "Eastern Partnership: The Next Five Years between Brussels and Moscow", Policy Paper No. 2, Association for International Affairs, Prague.

Lehne, S. (2014), "Time to Reset the European Neighbourhood Policy", Carnegie Endowment for International Peace, Washington, D.C., February.

Leigh, M. (2015), "The European Neighbourhood Policy: A suitable case for treatment", in S. Gstöhl and E. Lannon (eds), *The Neighbours of the Neighbours of the European Union's Neighbours: Diplomatic and Geopolitical Dimensions beyond the European Neighbourhood Policy*, 1st edition, Farnham: Ashgate Publishing Ltd.

Leonard, M. (2014), "Seven reasons why the Arab uprisings are eclipsing Western values", ECFR Commentary, European Council on Foreign Relations, 23 January.

Liik, L. (ed.) (2014), "Russia's 'Pivot' to Eurasia", European Council on Foreign Relations, London.

Maggi, E.-M. (2012), "A Leopard Can (Not) Change Its Spots: Promoting Environmental Policy in Morocco", in K. Böttger and T.A. Börzel (eds), *Policy Change in the EU's Immediate Neighbourhood: A Sectoral Approach*, Baden-Baden: Nomos, pp. 145-165.

Maggi, E.-M. (2016), *The Will of Change – European Neighborhood Policy, Domestic Actors and Institutional Change in Morocco*, Berlin: Springer.

Makarychev, A. and A. Devyatkov (2014), "The EU in Eastern Europe: Has Normative Power Become Geopolitical?", in PONARS Eurasia (ed.), *The Vilnius Moment*, 1st edition, PONARS Eurasia, George Washington University, Washington, D.C., pp. 1-5.

Mananashvili, S. (2015), "The Diffusion of the EU Asylum Acquis in the Eastern Neighbourhood: A Test for the EU's Normative Power", *European Foreign Affairs Review*, Vol. 20, No. 2, pp. 187–206.

Manoli, P. (2013), "Political Economy Aspects of Deep and Comprehensive Free Trade Agreements", *Eastern Journal of European Studies*, Vol. 4, No. 2, pp. 51-73.

Mattelaer, A. (2015), "The EU's Growing Engagement in the Sahel: From Development Aid to Military Coordination", in S. Gstöhl and E. Lannon (eds), *The neighbours of the European Union's neighbours: Diplomatic and geopolitical dimensions beyond the European neighbourhood policy*, 1st edition, Farnham: Ashgate Publishing Ltd.

Maurer, H. and L. Simao (2013), "From regional power to global power? The European Neighbourhood Policy after the Lisbon Treaty", in A. Boening, J. Kremer and A. Van Loon, *Global Power Europe – Vol. 1: Theoretical and Institutional Approaches to the EU's External Relations*, Berlin: Springer.

Mearsheimer, J.J. (2014), "Why the Ukraine Crisis Is the West's Fault: The Liberal Delusions That Provoked Putin", *Foreign Affairs*, Vol. 93, No. 5.

Merabishvili, G. (2015), "The EU and Azerbaijan: Game on for a more normative policy?", CEPS Policy Brief No. 329, Centre for European Policy Studies, Brussels, March.

Meister, S. (2013), "EU–Russia Relations and the Common Neighborhood: The Ball is on the EU's Side", DGAPanalyse No. 7, German Council on Foreign Relations, Berlin, August.

Meister, S. and J. Puglierin (2015), "Perception and Exploitation: Russia's Non-Military Influence in Europe", DGAPkompakt No. 10, German Council on Foreign Relations, Berlin, September.

Merkel, W. (2004), "Embedded and Defective Democracies", *Democratization*, Vol. 11, No. 5, pp. 33–58.

Mocanu, O. (2013), "Some considerations on the intergovernmental dimension of the European Neighbourhood Policy", *Eastern Journal of European Studies*, Vol. 4, No. 2, pp. 37-49.

Monaghan, A. (2015), "A 'New Cold War'? Abusing History, Misunderstanding Russia", Chatham House Research Paper, Chatham House, London, May.

Montalbano, P. and S. Nenci (2014), "Assessing the trade impact of the European Neighbourhood Policy on the EU-MED Free Trade Area", *Applied Economics*, Vol. 46, No. 7, pp. 730-740.

Montesano, F.S., T. Van der Togt and W. Zweers (2016), "The Europeanisation of Moldova: Is the EU on the Right Track?", Clingendael Report, Clingendael Netherlands Institute of International Relations, The Hague, July.

Morillas, P. (2015), "From Policies to Politics: The European Union as an International Mediator in the Mediterranean", IEMed Euromesco series, No. 23, European Institute of the Mediterranean, Barcelona, February.

Müller, P. (2016), "The revised European Neighbourhood policy and the EU's comprehensive approach towards the Israeli–Palestinian conflict: Not so new, after all", in D. Bouris and T. Schumacher (eds), *The Revised European Neighbourhood Policy: Continuity and Change in EU Foreign Policy*, Basingstoke: Palgrave Macmillan.

Najšlová, L., V. Řiháčková and O. Shumylo-Tapiola (2013), "The EU in the East: Too Ambitious in Rhetoric, too Unfocused in Action", Policy Paper No. 71, Notre Europe–Jacques Delors Institute, Paris and Berlin, February.

Natorski, M. (2016), "The EU and crisis in Ukraine: Policy continuity in times of disorder?", in D. Bouris and T. Schumacher (eds), *The Revised European Neighbourhood Policy: Continuity and Change in EU Foreign Policy*, Basingstoke: Palgrave Macmillan, pp. 177-196.

Navasardian, B. (2015), "Position Paper 1: Armenia", in F. Hett, S. Kikić and S. Meuser (eds), *Reassessing the European Neighbourhood Policy: The Eastern Dimension*, Friedrich-Ebert-Stiftung, Bonn, June.

Neuvonen, M. (2015), "Fear of Migration: Is the EU's Southern Neighbourhood Policy Fading Away?", FIIA Briefing Paper No. 177, Finnish Institute of International Affairs, Helsinki, June.

Nielsen, K. (2013), "EU Soft Power and the Capability-Expectations Gap", *Journal of Contemporary European Research*, Vol. 9, No. 5.

Nielsen, K.L. and M. Vilson (2014), "The Eastern Partnership: Soft Power Strategy or Policy Failure?", *European Foreign Affairs Review*, Vol. 19, No. 2, pp. 243-262.

Niktina, J. (2014), "Winning the Hearts of Eastern Partnership States", in PONARS Eurasia (ed.), *The Vilnius Moment*, 1st edition, PONARS Eurasia, George Washington University, Washington, D.C., pp. 10-14.

Nougayrède, N. (2015), "France and the Eastern Partnership: The view from Paris", European Council of Foreign Relations, May.

Orbie, J. and A. Wetzel (eds) (2015), *The substance of EU international democracy promotion*, Houndmills: Palgrave Macmillan.

Pace, M. (2014), "The EU's Interpretation of the 'Arab Uprisings': Understanding the Different Visions about Democratic Change in EU-MENA Relations", *Journal of Common Market Studies*, Vol. 52, No. 5, pp. 969-984.

Pardo, S. (2014), "Views from the Neighbourhood: Israel", in N. Chaban and M. Holland (eds), *Communicating Europe in Times of Crisis: External Perceptions of the European Union*, Basingstoke: Palgrave Macmillan.

Parkes, R. and A. Sobják (2014), "Understanding EU Action during 'Euromaidan': Lessons for the Next Phase", PISM Strategic File, No. 5 (41), Polish Institute of International Affairs, Warsaw, February.

Pech, L. (2012), "The Rule of Law as a Guiding Principle of European Union's External Action", CLEER Working Paper No. 2012/3, Centre for the Law of EU External Relations, The Hague.

Perthes, V. (2011), "Europe and the Arab Spring", *Survival*, Vol. 53, No. 6, pp. 73-84.

Petrov, R. (2012), "Energy Community as a promoter of the European Union's 'Energy Acquis' to its neighbourhood", *Legal Issues of Economic Integration*, Vol. 39, No. 3, pp. 331-356.

Petrova, I. and K. Raube (2016), "Euronest: What Drives Inter-Parliamentary Cooperation in the Eastern Partnership?", *European Foreign Affairs Review*, Vol. 21, No. 1, pp. 35–56.

Pieters, K. (2013), "Deep and comprehensive free trade agreements: Liberalisation of goods and services between the Mediterranean neighbours and the EU", CLEER Working Paper No. 2013/3, Centre for the Law of EU External Relations, The Hague.

Poli, S. (2016), *The European Neighbourhood Policy – Values and Principles*, Abingdon: Routledge.

PONARS Eurasia (2014*)*, *The Vilnius Moment*, PONARS Eurasia Policy Perspectives, George Washington University, Washington, D.C., March.

Popescu, N. (2012), *EU Foreign Policy and Post-Soviet Conflicts: Stealth Intervention*, Abingdon: Routledge.

Portela, C. (2012), "The EU sanctions operation in Syria: Conflict management by other means", UNISCI Discussion Paper No. 30, Singapore Management University, pp. 151-158.

Preiherman, Y. (2015), "Belarus and the European Neighbourhood Policy: A Special Case for 'a Special Case'", in J. Forbrig and A. Inayeh (eds), "Reviewing the European Neighbourhood Policy: Eastern Perspectives", Europe Policy Paper No. 4, German Marshall Fund of the United States, Washington, D.C.

Proedrou, F. (2016), "EU Energy Security beyond Ukraine: Towards Holistic Diversification", *European Foreign Affairs Review*, Vol. 21, No. 1, pp. 57-74.

Raik, K. (2012), "The EU and Mass Protests in the Neighbourhood: Models of Normative (In)action", *European Foreign Affairs Review*, Vol. 17, No. 4, pp. 553–575.

Raik, K., N. Helwig and J. Jokela (2014), "EU Sanctions against Russia: Europe Brings a Hard Edge to its Economic Power", FIIA Briefing Paper No. 162, Finnish Institute of International Affairs, Helsinki, October.

Rieker, P. (2014), "The European Neighbourhood Policy: An instrument for security community building", NUPI Working Paper No. 832, Norwegian Institute of International Affairs, Oslo.

Sadowski, R. (2013), "Partnership in times of crisis: Challenges for the Eastern European countries' integration with Europe", OSW Point of View No. 36, Centre for Eastern Studies, Warsaw, July.

Sagrera, R. (2014), "The Impact of Visa Liberalisation in Eastern Partnership Countries, Russia and Turkey on Trans-Border Mobility", CEPS Paper in Liberty and Security in Europe No. 63, Centre for European Policy Studies, Brussels, March.

Sakwa, R. (2016), *Frontline Ukraine: Crisis in the Borderlands*, London: I.B.Tauris.

Samokhvalov, V. (2015), "Ukraine between Russia and the European Union: Triangle Revisited", *Europe-Asia Studies*, Vol. 67, No. 9, pp. 1371-1393.

Sapir, A. and G. Zachmann (2011), "Eastern European lessons for the southern Mediterranean", Bruegel Policy Contribution No. 8, Bruegel, Brussels, July.

Sasse, G. (2013), "Linkages and the promotion of democracy: The EU's eastern neighbourhood", *Democratization*, Vol. 20. No. 4, pp. 553-591.

Scheller, B., N. Baalbaki and A. Molter (2016), "Views from the South – The European Neighbourhood Policy in Lebanon", Heinrich Böll Stiftung European Union, Brussels, September.

Schimmelfennig, F. (2012), "Europeanization beyond Europe", *Living Reviews in European Governance*, Vol. 7, No. 1, pp. 1-31.

Schumacher, T. (2011), "The EU and the Arab Spring: Between Spectatorship and Actorness", *Insight Turkey*, Vol. 13, No. 3, pp. 107-119.

Schumacher, T. (2012), "Conditionality, differentiation, regionality and the 'new' ENP in the light of Arab Revolts", in E. Barbé and A. Herranz-Surrallés (eds), *The Challenge of Differentiation in Euro-Mediterranean Relations: Flexible Regional Cooperation or Fragmentation*, London and New York: Routledge, pp. 142-158.

Schumacher, T. (2016a), "Back to the Future: The 'New' ENP towards the Southern Neighbourhood and the End of Ambition", CEBOP No. 1, College of Europe, Bruges, January.

Schumacher, T. (2016b), *Differentiation in EU–Neighbourhood Relations*, Euromed Survey No. 6: Qualitative Analysis, European Institute of the Mediterranean, Barcelona.

Seeberg, P. (2014), "Strategic Patience and EU Reform-Support: EU and the 'Arab Spring': The State of Play after Three Years", *European Foreign Affairs Review*, Vol. 19, No. 3, pp. 453–470.

Sek, A. (2013), "EEAS Audit in the Eastern Neighbourhood: To What Extent Have the New Treaty Provisions Delivered?", IAI Paper No. 13/10, Istituto Affari Internazionali, Rome.

Shapovalova, N. (2013), "Visa-free travel for the EU's Eastern partners: Time to act", FRIDE Policy Brief No. 165, FRIDE, Madrid.

Shapovalova, N. (2015), "How can the Eastern Partnership Civil Society Forum strengthen its advocacy function?", Paper commissioned by the Eastern Partnership Civil Society Forum.

Shapovalova, N. and R. Youngs (2012), "EU democracy promotion in the Eastern neighbourhood: A turn to civil society?", FRIDE Working Paper No. 115, FRIDE, Madrid.

Shepherd, R., I. Gyarmati, Z. Hesová and P. Sasnal (2013), "What role for the Visegrad countries on the Mediterranean coast?", Policy Brief, Central European Policy Institute, Bratislava.

Sherr, J. (2015), *The New East–West Discord: Russian Objectives, Western Interests*, Clingendael Report, Clingendael Netherlands Institute of International Relations, The Hague, December.

Sivitski, A. (2015), "Position Paper 3: Belarus", in F. Hett, S. Kikić and S. Meuser (eds), *Reassessing the European Neighbourhood Policy: The Eastern Dimension*, Friedrich-Ebert-Stiftung, Berlin, June.

Skorupska, A. (2014), "Building Awareness about the EU in Ukraine", PISM Bulletin, No. 68 (773), Polish Institute of International Affairs, Warsaw, May.

Slavkova, L. and A. Shirinyan (eds) (2015), *Unrewarding Crossroads: The Black Sea Region between the EU and Russia*, Foundation Sofia Platform, Sofia.

Soimu, O., V. Trofimov and L. Gomez-Urquijo (2012), "European Neighborhood Policy: Some Conclusions in a Country-specific Framing", *Review of International Comparative Management*, Vol. 13, No. 1, pp. 130-140.

Soler i Lecha, E. and L. Tarragona (2015), "Self-imposed Limitations: Why is the EU losing relevance in the Mediterranean", CIDOB notes, No. 23, Barcelona Centre for International Affairs, Barcelona, February.

Solodkyy, S. and V. Sharlay (2015), "How could the EU accelerate reform in Ukraine?", Institute of World Policy, Kiev, November.

Solonenko, I. (with H. Hallgren) (2015), "Can the European Union Help Ukraine to Succeed? Reforms, the Russian Factor and Implications for the Eastern Neighbourhood", Heinrich Böll Stiftung European Union, Brussels.

Stewart, S. (2011), "EU Democracy Promotion in the Eastern Neighbourhood: One Template, Multiple Approaches", *European Foreign Affairs Review*, Vol. 16, No. 5.

Tagliapietra, S. and G. Zachmann (2016), "Energy across the Mediterranean: A call for realism", Bruegel Policy Brief No. 3, Bruegel, Brussels, April.

Techau, J. (2014), "Why the EU Will Fail as Ukraine's Guarantor", Blog Post, Carnegie Europe, Brussels, 16 September.

Telo, M. (2013), "The EU: A Civilian Power's Diplomatic Action after the Lisbon Treaty: Bridging Internal Complexity and International Convergence", in M. Telo and F. Ponjaert (eds), *The EU's Foreign Policy: What Kind of Power and Diplomatic Action?*, 1st edition, Abingdon: Routledge, pp. 27-63.

Thépaut, C. (2011), "Can the EU Pressure Dictators? Reforming ENP Conditionality after the Arab Spring", EU Diplomacy Paper No. 6, College of Europe, Bruges.

Thomas, D.C. (2012), "Still Punching below its Weight? Coherence and Effectiveness in European Union Foreign Policy", *Journal of Common Market Studies*, Vol. 50, No. 3, pp. 457-474.

Thompson, J. (2015), "The Global Players in the EU's Broader Neighbourhood", in S. Gstöhl and E. Lannon (eds), *The neighbours of the European Union's neighbours: Diplomatic and geopolitical dimensions beyond the European neighbourhood policy*, 1st edition, Farnham: Ashgate Publishing Ltd.

Tocci, N. (2007), "Can the EU Promote Democracy and Human Rights through the ENP? The Case for Refocusing on the Rule of Law", in M. Cremona and G Meloni (eds), *The European Neighbourhood Policy: A New Framework for Modernisation?*, EUI Working Papers, LAW 21, European University Institute, Florence, pp. 23-35.

Tocci, N. (2014), "The Neighbourhood Policy is Dead. What's Next for European Foreign Policy Along its Arc of Instability?", IAI Working Paper No. 14, Istituto Affari Internazionali, Rome, November.

Tömmel, I. (2013), "The new neighbourhood policy of the EU: An appropriate response to the Arab Spring?", *Democracy and Security*, Vol. 9, No. 2, pp. 19–39.

Trenin, D. (2016), "A Five-Year Outlook for Russian Foreign Policy: Demands, Drivers, and Influences", White Paper, Carnegie Moscow Centre, Moscow, March.

Van der Loo, G. (2014), "The EU-Ukraine Deep and Comprehensive Free Trade Area: a coherent mechanism for legislative approximation?", in P. Van Elsuwege and R. Petrov (eds), *Legislative Approximation and Application of EU Law in the Eastern Neighbourhood of the European Union: Towards a Common Regulatory Space?*, Abingdon: Routledge, pp. 63-88.

Van der Loo, G. (2016a), *The EU-Ukraine association agreement and deep and comprehensive free trade area: A new legal instrument for EU integration without membership?*, Leiden and Boston: Brill/Nijhoff.

Van der Loo, G. (2016b), "Mapping out the Scope and Contents of the DCFTAs with Tunisia and Morocco", IEMed Euromesco series, No. 28, European Institute of the Mediterranean, Barcelona.

Van der Loo, G. and P. Van Elsuwege (2012), "Competing Paths of Regional Economic Integration in the Post-Soviet Space: Legal and Political Dilemmas for Ukraine", *Review of Central and East European Law*, Vol. 37, No. 4, pp. 421-447.

Van der Loo, G., P. Van Elsuwege and R. Petrov (2014), "The EU-Ukraine Association Agreement: Assessment of an Innovative Legal Instrument", EUI Working Paper, LAW 2014/09, European University Institute, Florence.

Van Elsuwege, P. and G. Van der Loo (2016), "Continuity and change in the legal relations between the EU and its neighbours: A result of path dependency and spill-over effects", in D. Bouris and T. Schumacher (eds), *The Revised European Neighbourhood Policy: Continuity and Change in EU Foreign Policy*, Basingstoke: Palgrave Macmillan, pp. 97-116.

Van Elsuwege, P. and O. Burlyuk (2016), "Exporting the rule of law to the EU's Eastern Neighbourhood: Reconciling coherence and differentiation", in S. Poli (ed.), *The European Neighbourhood Policy – Values and Principles*, London and New York: Routledge, pp. 167–182.

Van Elsuwege, P. and R. Petrov (2011), "Article 8 TEU: Towards a New Generation of Agreements with the Neighbouring Countries of the European Union", *European Law Review*, Vol. 36, No. 5, pp. 688-703.

Van Elsuwege, P. and R. Petrov (2014), *Legislative Approximation and Application of EU Law in the Eastern Neighbourhood of the European Union: Towards a Common Regulatory Space?*, Abingdon: Routledge.

Van Hüllen, V. (2012), "The European Union and Democracy Promotion in the Mediterranean: Strategic Choices after the Arab Spring", in K. Böttger and T.A. Börzel (eds), *Policy Change in the EU's Immediate Neighbourhood: A Sectoral Approach*, Baden-Baden: Nomos, pp. 119-144.

Van Vooren, B. (2012), *EU External Relations Law and the European Neighbourhood Policy: A Paradigm for Coherence*, Abingdon: Routledge.

Völkel, J.C. (2014), "More for More, Less for Less – More or Less: A Critique of the EU's Arab Spring Response à la Cinderella", *European Foreign Affairs Review*, Vol. 19, No. 2, pp. 263–282.

Von Bogdandy, A. (2010), "Founding Principles", in A. Von Bogdandy and J. Bast (eds), *Principles of European Constitutional Law*, 2nd edition, Oxford: Hart Publishing, pp. 11-54, 22.

Walton-Roberts, M. and J. Hennebry (2014), *Territoriality and Migration in the EU: Spilling over the Wall*, Dordrecht, Heidelberg, New York and London: Springer.

Wesslau, F. (2016), "Will the EU prolong Economic Sanctions against Russia?", European Council on Foreign Relations, 16 May.

Wetzel, A. (2016), "From halt to hurry: External and domestic influences on Ukrainian asylum policy", *Eurasian Geography and Economics*, Vol. 57, No. 1, pp. 66-88.

Wetzel, A. and J. Orbie (2012), "The EU's Promotion of External Democracy: In Search of the Plot", CEPS Policy Brief No. 281, Centre for European Policy Studies, Brussels, September.

Wetzel, A. and J. Orbie (2015), "Comparing Country Cases: Output-Oriented EU Democracy Promotion?", in J. Orbie and A. Wetzel (eds) (2015), *The substance of EU international democracy promotion*, Houndmills: Palgrave Macmillan, pp. 235-254.

Wiśniewski, P.D. (2013), "The Eastern Partnership – It is High Time to Start a Real 'Partnership'", Carnegie Endowment for International Peace, Moscow, November.

Witney, N. and A. Dworkin (2012), "A Power Audit of EU–North Africa Relations", European Council on Foreign Relations, September.

Whitman, R. and A. Juncos (2012), "The Arab Spring, the Eurozone Crisis and the Neighbourhood: A Region in Flux", *Journal of Common Market Studies*, Vol. 50, pp.147-161.

Wolczuk, K. (2011), "Perceptions of, and Attitudes towards, the Eastern Partnership amongst the Partner Countries' Political Elites", *Eastern Partnership Review*, No. 5, December.

Wolczuk, K. (2016), "Managing the flows of gas and rules: Ukraine between the EU and Russia", *Eurasian Geography and Economics*, Vol. 57, No. 1, pp. 113-137.

Wouters, J. and S. Duquet (2013), "The Arab Uprisings and the European Union: In search of a comprehensive strategy", Working Paper No. 98, Leuven Centre for Global Governance Studies, Leuven, January.

Wouters, J., G. De Baere, B. Van Vooren, K. Raube, J. Odermatt, T. Ramopoulos, T. Van Der Sanden and Y. Tanghe (2013), "The Organization and Functioning of the European External Action Service: Achievements, Challenges and Opportunities", EXPO/B/AFET/2012/07, European Parliament, Directorate-General for External Policies of the Union.

Youngs, R. (2015), "The European Endowment for Democracy, Two Years on", Carnegie Europe, Brussels, September.

Zagorski, A. (2011), "Eastern Partnership from the Russian Perspective", IPG No. 3/2011, Internationale Politik und Gesellschaft, Berlin, pp. 41-61.

Zaiotti, R. (2007), "Of Friends and Fences: Europe's Neighbourhood Policy and the 'Gated Community Syndrome'", *European Integration*, Vol. 29, No. 2, pp. 143-162.

Zajac, J. (2015), "The EU in the Mediterranean: Between Its International Identity and Member States' Interests'", *European Foreign Affairs Review*, Vol. 20, No. 1, pp. 65-82.

Zulaika, C. (2012), "State of Play: The EU, the African Parties to the Cotonou Agreement and the ENP", in S. Gstöhl and E. Lannon (eds), *The neighbours of the European Union's neighbours: Diplomatic and geopolitical dimensions beyond the European neighbourhood policy*, 1st edition, Farnham: Ashgate Publishing Ltd.

www.ingramcontent.com/pod-product-compliance
Lightning Source LLC
Chambersburg PA
CBHW030651270326
41929CB00007B/317